FOCUSING
MY GAZE

FOCUSING MY GAZE

*Beholding the
Upward, Inward, Outward
Mission of Jesus*

MAX WILKINS

 Seedbed

Scripture quotations are taken from the Holy Bible, New
International Version®, NIV® Copyright © 1973, 1978, 1984,
2011 by Biblica, Inc.™ Used by permission of Zondervan.
All rights reserved worldwide. www.zondervan.com The
"NIV" and "New International Version" are trademarks
registered in the United States Patent and Trademark
Office by Biblica, Inc.™ All rights reserved worldwide.

Scripture quotations marked HCSB®, are taken from the Holman
Christian Standard Bible®, Copyright © 1999, 2000, 2002, 2003,
2009 by Holman Bible Publishers. Used by permission. HCSB®
is a federally registered trademark of Homan Bible Publishers.

Scripture quotations marked NKJV™ are taken from the
New King James Version®. Copyright © 1982 by Thomas
Nelson, Inc. Used by permission. All rights reserved.

Printed in the United States of America

Cover design by Strange Last Name
Page design and layout by PerfecType, Nashville, Tennessee

Wilkins, Max, 1960-
Focusing my gaze : beholding the upward, inward, outward mission of
Jesus / Max Wilkins. – Franklin, Tennessee : Seedbed Publishing, ©2021.

pages ; cm

ISBN 9781628248135 (paperback)
ISBN 9781628248258 (Mobi)
ISBN 9781628248265 (ePub)
ISBN 9781628248814 (uPDF)
OCLC 1249099246

1. Jesus Christ--Example. 2. Christian life.   3. Kingdom of God.
4. Bible. Isaiah, VI--Criticism, interpretation, etc.   I. Title.

BT304.2.W54 2021   248.4   2021938147

 Seedbed

SEEDBED PUBLISHING
Franklin, Tennessee
seedbed.com

This book is dedicated to the following people, without whom neither my life of faith nor this work itself would have ever been possible:

To my parents, Bill and Linda Wilkins, who have nurtured me in love and faith, supported me in life and ministry, and encouraged me repeatedly through the years to write a book. Thank you for your patience. It is finally here.

To my wife, Dorothy "Dee Dee" Wilkins, whose name literally means "the gift of God." You have always lived up to your name. The constant support and encouragement you have given me through the years are only surpassed by the patience you have shown and the sacrifices you have made for the sake of helping me live out my calling. I love you.

To my covenant group, "The Jengas": Jorge Acevedo, Matthew Hartsfield, Doug Kokx, Dale Locke, Joe MacLaren, and Wayne Wiatt. For thirty years we have shared deeply the joys and sorrows, the victories and challenges of life and ministry. Thank you for loving me, encouraging me, challenging me, and holding me accountable. I love doing life with you guys and I can't imagine doing it without you.

CONTENTS

The Focus of My Gaze

Therefore, since we are surrounded by such a great cloud of witnesses, let us throw off everything that hinders and the sin that so easily entangles. And let us run with perseverance the race marked out for us, fixing our eyes on Jesus, the pioneer and perfecter of faith. For the joy set before him he endured the cross, scorning its shame, and sat down at the right hand of the throne of God.

—HEBREWS 12:1–2

The focus of my gaze will determine the state of my being. Where I fix my eyes, my attention, my concentration, and my awareness will, in large part, shape what my life is about.

My gaze will also influence nearly everything in my life. It will have a pronounced impact on my relationships. It will deeply affect the overall direction of my life, as well as the outcomes. It will sway my emotions and guide my decisions. All these things will effectively be true regardless of who or what I choose as my focus. There are some choices that will lead to life and others that only lead to destruction, darkness, and death. Fortunately, every human being has the power to choose the focus of their gaze.

Jesus

This is a book about Jesus. Unabashedly so.

I love Jesus deeply. If you don't already love Him, I still hope that you will read this book. In doing so, I hope you will fall in love with Him as well. From the outset, I want to be clear that of all the people, or places, or things that you could choose as the focus of your gaze, Jesus is, by far, the best choice. In saying "the focus of your gaze," however, I am not suggesting an occasional glance in His direction. I mean making Jesus your North Star, your life GPS, and your source of attraction, wonder, and awe. If you are uncertain what a life like that would even look like, read on. This book will attempt to take you there.

The book of Hebrews 11 is sometimes referred to as God's "Hall of Faith." The entire chapter is filled with stories of people who lived profound lives of faith and faithfulness. Some of those named are quite famous. Others lived and died largely anonymously. Some of them had the kind of success the world glorifies and applauds. Others lived quite tragic lives, and died with very little in the way of earthly success. What they all had in common, however, was a deep and life-changing faith relationship with their Maker, and the promise of eternal life with Him. Hebrews suggests that whatever trade-offs they may have experienced in this life, they all ultimately chose well.

In light of this Hall of Faith, this "great cloud of witnesses," the author of Hebrews then says to all of us, "let us throw off everything that hinders and the sin that so easily entangles. And let us run with perseverance the race marked out for us, fixing our eyes on Jesus, the pioneer and perfecter of faith" (Heb. 12:1–2a). In every life there are those things that hinder us, and the sin that so easily entangles us. At times it is essential that we focus on those things. We will find that in the light of God's glory, not only is this focus helpful, albeit painful, it is also part of God's good news for us. As we invite the Lord to show us what is hindering us, and to expose the sin that is robbing us of life, we also find the power and ability to break free of these things—to literally throw them off.

More important, however, this book will discuss how we can "fix our eyes on Jesus." We will see why He is the author of our faith, the one who goes before us, who brings us the gift of faith, and who makes a way for us to receive that gift. And we will learn not only why, but how He is the perfecter, or finisher, of our faith. We will discover that as we fix our eyes on Him and cooperate with His grace, He is able to fulfill His promises in our lives. Not only are those promises trustworthy and true, they are also truly wonderful.

The Kingdom of God

The book is about the kingdom of God.

Although God's kingdom is a subject we rarely hear about in the churches today, it is a central focus of Jesus and His ministry. Well more than one hundred times in our gospel stories, Jesus speaks of the kingdom of God. John the Baptist, in preparing the way for Jesus' ministry, said, "Repent, for the kingdom of heaven has come near" (Matt. 3:2). Later, Jesus reported: "'The time has come,' he said. 'The kingdom of God has come near. Repent and believe the good news!'" (Mark 1:15). And when His followers questioned how and where to encounter this kingdom, Jesus told them: "nor will people say, 'Here it is,' or 'There it is,' because the kingdom of God is in your midst" (Luke 17:21). The good news of Jesus' earthly ministry was the coming of the kingdom.

Jesus makes an incredible promise about the kingdom. When I first began following Him in late 1980, I thought I should read the stories of Jesus in the Bible. I had just experienced a rather dramatic encounter with the Lord (you can read about it in chapter 6) and given my life to Him. I wanted to know all I could know about this Lord I had trusted. I began reading Matthew's gospel because it was first in the New Testament. I was rolling along just fine until I got to chapter 6. Right in the middle of His famous Sermon on the Mount, Jesus was speaking about all the things we want and need in life, and how we worry and fret over those things and struggle to receive them. He pointed out that birds and flowers don't struggle after these things; they simply receive them from God. Then He said something I found incredible: "But seek first his kingdom and his righteousness, and all these things will be given to you as well" (Matt. 6:33).

I read these words over and over several times. I had only been following Jesus for a few days. I had promised Him that if He would show me His will in my life, I would do it. But this statement just seemed like too much to me. Jesus appeared to be saying that I needed to focus my gaze on His kingdom, and on His righteousness (and thus, on Him), and that, in doing so, all the other things I was seeking would be given to me. I had a very early crisis of faith. My immediate, immature, and irresponsible response was to force-fully close my Bible, look into the heavens, and declare: "I just don't believe this is true." Today, I can see how impulsive and uninformed my response was, but that evening that is exactly how I felt.

The idea of following Jesus didn't trouble me. Seeking first His kingdom actually seemed like a good idea. Even laying everything else aside was something I considered a small price to pay. I had trusted Him with my life, and I didn't want to go back to being in charge. It was just that there were things I wanted, and thought I needed, and I wasn't sure how seeking His kingdom and His righteousness would lead to me having them. Things like a wife to be my life mate and a job and career through which I might find meaning. Even silly things, such as being in a movie. (I fancied myself movie-star material. Apparently, I didn't focus my gaze on too many mirrors.) I had a long list. I was not trying to back out on my promise to the Lord. Though I was still committed to following Him, I literally said out loud to the Lord, "I am laying all of this stuff down, for You. I will try to seek first Your kingdom and Your righteousness. But I just don't see how that will lead to 'all these things.'" And, although Scripture says we should "not put the Lord [our] God to the test" (Luke 4:12), in God's grace and mercy, I now believe God received that outburst from me as a challenge, and set about to show me I was wrong.

It was more than a decade later, as I was driving off the set of a movie in which I had landed a small role (long story for another day), that I heard the gentle, loving, quiet voice of the Lord simply say, "You thought I forgot about the movie, didn't you?" I pulled my car over to the side of the road as emotion swept over me and I began to weep. I had long since forgotten my juvenile list, and my faithless reaction to God's promise. But God had not forgotten. In that moment it occurred to me that while I had been attempting to seek first His kingdom and His righteousness, the Lord had indeed brought every one of the things on my list into my life.

The point is not that God wanted me to be a movie star. He didn't, and I'm definitely not. But God wants us to trust that He is infinitely able to bring His word to bear in our lives and to see His promises fulfilled. I continue to fix my gaze on Jesus and on His kingdom, and God continues to show me the wonders of His kingdom.

When the author of Hebrews encourages us to fix our eyes on Jesus, he writes: "For the joy set before him [Jesus] endured the cross" (Heb. 12:2b). What was the joy set before Him, so clearly the focus of His gaze? I am convinced it was a threefold joy.

- First, the joy of hearing his heavenly Father say, "Well done, good and faithful servant!" (Matt. 25:21a). There is no doubt that Jesus' gaze was firmly fixed on His Father.
- Second, the joy of knowing His kingdom would come and His will would be done on earth as it is in heaven (see Matthew 6:10). I believe Jesus could see the consummation of the kingdom, and kept His focus there.
- Finally, I believe it was the joy of knowing that by enduring the cross, He was once and for all

paying the price for the sins of humanity, making a gracious way for our relationship with God to be restored and for the image of God to be renewed in us.

Jesus' gaze was fixed on God the Father, His kingdom, and His children. And because He sat down on that throne, having endured the cross and been raised to new life, we are now encouraged to fix our gaze upon Him (see Hebrews 12:2)!

Abundant Life

This is a book about life—*abundant* life—the life we were created to live.

Shortly after my Matthew 6:33 meltdown, I continued to read the Gospels. When I got to John, I discovered another promise of Jesus, and this time I didn't doubt. I wanted to believe it. I needed to believe it. I did believe it. And it has become my life verse for forty years: "The thief comes only to steal and kill and destroy; I have come that they may have life, and have it to the full" (John 10:10).

As you will read in chapter 6, I already knew a good bit about the thieves who come to steal our dreams, kill our joy, and destroy our lives. I had danced with them until they almost won. But now here was Jesus saying that He had come to give me life to the full. I wanted that life and I wanted it to the full!

There are a number of words in the Greek language for "life." Some mean bodily life, the act of breathing in and out. Others, the opposite of death. But in John 10:10, the word for life is *zoe*. This Greek term doesn't simply mean existing, or breathing in and out. It describes life in the sense of aliveness, an appetite for life, a zest for living. It is about squeezing everything God has to offer out of this gift of life. It infers a joyous celebration of life itself. And it is this life that Jesus says He came to give us.

When the verse speaks of having that life "to the full," some have falsely used these words to imply that those who trust Jesus should expect material blessing, big houses, and fancy cars. Although God may choose to bless some people in that way, the term Jesus uses in this promise is a qualitative term, not a quantitative one. He is not saying that if we have enough faith the Lord will buy us a Lexus! He is saying that not only will the Lord give us an aliveness and a zest for living, but also lives of the highest quality. In essence, He is promising us the lives we were created to live.

I will never forget Mrs. Routson. I was in seminary, training to be a pastor. One semester, as part of my practical ministry studies, I was assigned as chaplain to a floor of a local nursing home. I visited Mrs. Routson's room on my first day. I was unprepared for what I would discover there.

She was the victim of a stroke. A very large woman, the stroke had left her unable to move anything on her body except her left arm and her head. Completely bedridden, she spent her entire day in a specially designed gel bed that constantly jiggled in order to prevent bed sores. Mrs. Routson had been in the bed for so long that her body had pooled into the middle, and the surface of her exposed skin had taken on a hard, leathery look. To feed herself she was forced to spoon food off a tray, hold it up over her open mouth, and attempt to drop it in. Often, she missed. When

I entered the room for the first time, she had just finished lunch. The sight that greeted me looked unlike any person I had ever seen before. In my surprise, I almost let out a gasp and fled. I have always been glad that I did not.

A smile broke across her food-stained face, and Mrs. Routson laughed a friendly greeting: "I'm sorry. I must look a mess. I've just finished my lunch. Can you help me wipe off my face?" I was happy to do so. Then she extended her left hand through the hospital bed railing and introduced herself. Thus began a relationship with a remarkable woman.

Mrs. Routson always seemed to be having a good day. Though she never left her bed, rarely had visitors, and had almost no prospect of recovery from her stroke, she was living a joy-filled life. She had a well-worn Bible on her nightstand. When I visited, she regularly regaled me with whatever parts of the Bible she had read that morning. And whether that was something as exciting as the adventures of King David or something as dry as the "begats," when Mrs. Routson told them, the stories came to life. She told me once that she had read the entire Bible cover to cover thirty-nine times, and she was going for forty. "It never gets old," she said.

She loved old comedy movies and Westerns on the television, and would laugh like a schoolgirl at slapstick comedy. She animatedly shared with me the stories of her children and the grandchildren who were growing up out of state. One day she showed me a picture her little five-year-old granddaughter had drawn. "Isn't that beautiful?" she asked. I looked at the picture and couldn't figure out what it was supposed to be. It looked like some kind of an arch, with an arm coming out and a heart shape near the hand. Finally, as I struggled to make sense of what I was seeing, Mrs. Routson explained: "Don't you see? It's me! My granddaughter is too small to see over the rail of the bed. So, when she is standing here, I just put my arm out, and she holds my hand. She drew me as she sees me. I think it is beautiful."

When Halloween rolled around, the nursing home arranged to have some children come through in costume, going door-to-door to collect candy. Mrs. Routson asked me if I could help her get ready. I was uncertain how to explain to her that I wasn't sure the children would understand her situation. Sensing my hesitation, she said brightly, "Oh, Max, I know the children don't need to come in here. Just put some candy in a bowl by the door. I will enjoy hearing them stop by and get some." We did exactly that. The next time I visited, Mrs. Routson couldn't wait to tell me all about it.

One day, after several months of daily visiting with this remarkable lady—visits filled with laughter, stories, and joy—I asked her about her life. "You have so many challenges, and so much you could complain about, and yet you always seem so alive and joyous. Why do you think that is?"

"Oh, Max," she said, "there is just so much good in my life. I love Jesus and He has been so good to me. He has filled my life with so many wonderful things. If I get to feeling a bit down, I just look to Him, and I remember how much He loves me, and what He has done for me. And I think about all the blessings I have. I consider what He is preparing for me. And when I'm looking to Him, the problems just seem to fade away, and all that's left is the good stuff."

Mrs. Routson passed away a few weeks later. I have no doubt that she is already experiencing all that her Lord prepared for her for eternity. But I am so grateful that she didn't wait until heaven to experience the abundant life the Lord had for her all along. And I will always be grateful that part of the abundant life the Lord had for me was meeting Mrs. Routson.

The Lord wants each of us to experience that same abundant life, now and for eternity.

The Four Looks

Oddly enough, for a book about Jesus, this entire journey will be framed by the prophet Isaiah's encounter with the Lord as described in Isaiah 6. In that unique and wonderful event, we will see how the Lord takes Isaiah through all the major moves of a holy life. This God-encounter in Isaiah's life has four separate looks, all of which are important for those who would like to discover and experience the abundant life the Lord came to give us.

We will see how Isaiah:

- Looked up—and saw the glory of the Lord.
- Looked inward—and saw the true state of human beings, himself included.
- Looked outward—and saw the grace of the Lord.
- Looked around—and saw the mission of the Lord. He recognized both the need and his own true purpose.

Let's look!

ONE

The Upward Look

In the year that King Uzziah died, I saw the Lord, high and exalted, seated on a throne; and the train of his robe filled the temple.

—Isaiah 6:1

Can you imagine what must have been running through Isaiah's mind on that fateful day? The temple, God's chosen dwelling place among His people, began to shake with a violence normally associated with earthquakes. As both the doorposts and Isaiah's legs continued to tremble, his nostrils were overwhelmed with the fragrant smoke of incense wafting through the temple. Suddenly his ears hear the loud cries of seraphim flying around the room, and with the train of the Lord's robe gathering at his feet, Isaiah looks up and sees the Lord! And even as the seraphim announce and praise the holiness of God, they also celebrate God's glory. Indeed, they continually proclaim a remarkable truth: the whole earth is full of His glory! Staring into that glory unveiled,

Isaiah is, perhaps for the first time, about to see everything as it really is!

I have to admit, every time I read the words of Isaiah 6, I find myself just a bit envious of the prophet's experience. How awesome, in the most literal sense of the word, must it have been to see the Lord high and exalted? Abraham and Noah heard the voice of God. Moses witnessed the burning bush and, later, a glimpse of God's glory. Ezekiel saw angelic beings that are hard to even imagine. But all of these God-encounters pale in comparison to Isaiah's vision. He sees the Lord, hears the Lord, breathes the Lord, interacts with the Lord, and, in the process, he is transformed. How wonderful to experience this vision firsthand!

In the midst of my unhealthy envy of Isaiah, I often wonder: *What if God fully intended each of us to have experiences like Isaiah's, perhaps even regularly? What if Isaiah's experience depended more on Isaiah, and his actions, than on anything unusual from God? What if experiences such as Isaiah's were available to each of us, regularly, even daily?* It might surprise you to know that I believe God actually intended for glory encounters to be normative in the lives of all of His children, though perhaps not in the way we initially imagine.

In a small discipleship group that met in our home for years, we began each meeting by asking for reports of glory sightings from the members of the group. The idea was to share where we had seen and experienced the glory of God in our lives during the previous week. Initially, many in the group found this to be a difficult exercise. Often there would be long periods of embarrassed silence. It wasn't that the members of the group doubted the presence of God in our world, nor that His glory was visible in our lives. Instead, we soon came to realize that despite our belief that God's glory was present, we often spent our lives ignoring what God was doing and missing His glory. Once we began to regularly seek His glory, our reports of glory sightings became frequent, exciting, and the most encouraging part of our gatherings.

As I have contemplated Isaiah's encounter over the years, I've arrived at an important if not astounding biblical insight: Isaiah saw the Lord because he was looking for the Lord! Although this simple statement may seem self-evident, it is an easily overlooked reality. The truth is, human beings generally see what they are looking for. That is, in part, what Jesus meant in the Sermon on the Mount when He said, "Ask [and keep on asking] and it will be given to you; seek [and keep on seeking] and you will find" (Matt. 7:7a). God is not hiding. God desires to be seen by those who seek Him. Indeed, He later says to Jeremiah, "You will seek me and find me when you seek me with all your heart" (Jer. 29:13).

Isaiah saw things many of us long to see. Have you ever wished God would speak so clearly to you that it was undeniably His voice? Or longed for a glimpse of His face? Or even wished for a burning bush of your own? Many have. For Isaiah, the longings became reality. He saw the Lord because he looked for the Lord. And in sharing the details of his experience with us, Isaiah also gives us insight into how we might have similar God-encounters. Let's look closely at his report.

When the Crisis Comes

The story begins with the death of King Uzziah. This historical detail is more than a simple time stamp. The death of King Uzziah was a major, life-changing event for the people of Judah. Uzziah had been on the throne for fifty-two years, reigning over one of the most peaceful, productive, and prosperous seasons of Judah's history. In addition to his military prowess and wise economic policies, Uzziah also sought the Lord faithfully throughout his lifetime. Under the tutelage of a prophet named Zechariah, the king was able to bring the people of Judah back to God, and to the proper worship of God. As a result of his leadership and his reforms, the Lord blessed the people and the land. It was commonly said during Uzziah's reign that these were the greatest days of Judah since the reign of King Solomon.

To get a sense of having the same leader for fifty-two years, try to envision President Lyndon Johnson still being president of the United States in 2020! Whole generations would never have known another leader. Consider the anxiety the people must have experienced while living in the last days of this fifty-two-year reign of Uzziah. Then suddenly they receive the news that their king is dead. It had to have been extremely unsettling for the people of Judah.

In seasons of great change, many people become anxious and troubled. Often there is panic. Uncertainty about what is to come abounds. And we've all experienced situations where a beloved, respected leader has passed away, or moved on, only to be replaced by someone who makes a mess of everything. Indeed, in Judah, these very fears and uncertainties would soon prove to have been well-founded. Nevertheless, it is right in the middle of all of the confusion, anxiety, and uncertainty of this season that Isaiah sees the Lord. Because while others were panicking and frantically searching for answers, Isaiah looked up—and saw God!

Do you ever have times of worry in your life? Have you ever gone through seasons where you thought "life doesn't look so bright right now"? Have you ever had anxiety about what lies around the next corner? If you have children, do you worry about what the future holds for them? Of course you have. Everyone experiences these thoughts and feelings at times. The more important questions are: In times of uncertainty and doubt, where do we focus our gaze? Do we look to God? And even if we believe God wants to be seen by us, do we truly believe we can find Him?

The Whole Earth

"The whole earth is full of his glory" (Isa. 6:3), the seraphim proclaim. What an amazing revelation. Have you ever really considered what this proclamation by the angels implies? If the whole earth is full of the glory of God, where can we possibly be that is absent of God's glory? Consider this: the whole earth (that means pretty much everywhere) is full of (that means there is no place left to fill in) God's glory (not just good things, or beauty, or even good people, but literally the glory of the living God). Do you know what that means? Have you ever thought about it? If the whole earth is full of the glory of God, it means there is no place you can go, there is nothing you can be doing, there is no set of problems so deep, no challenge so great, that you are apart from the glory of God. Wherever you are, however dismal things may appear, whatever is going on, God is there . . . you only need to look. And if you look and God's glory is not in front of you, look beside you or around you. Seek Him. He wants to be found by you. But you will not find Him most times if you are not looking for Him.

Many years ago, I was preparing to preach at New Hope Christian Fellowship in Oahu, Hawaii (because someone has to suffer for Jesus in Hawaii!). During the worship time, as we were singing "I'm Desperate for You," the tech crew had projected an image of the face of Jesus on the front wall of the worship space. I looked at the image and was deeply drawn to it as I sang. Then I closed my eyes for a minute and when I opened them again, the image was gone! I remember thinking, *No! Wait! Bring it back. I want to see His face some more.* But just as I was thinking this, I looked to the side and there was the image again, this time on the side wall. It wasn't gone at all; it had just moved. And in a few minutes the image moved again, this time back to its original location. In creatively presenting the worship experience, the tech team ensured that the face of Jesus never left our worship space, but it wasn't always in the same place. I remember being comforted by that realization. It seemed to bear out something vitally important. While the Lord doesn't leave us or forsake us, and while His glory fills the whole earth, we are sometimes required to look for His face in order to see and experience His presence. I know it was just an image on a screen at New Hope, but in our spiritual lives it is more than that. Because no matter where we are in this life, no matter what it going on, no matter how severe our problems or how deep our worries, the Lord is there. The Lord is right in the midst of us.

There is a beautiful verse in Habakkuk 2. The prophet is speaking of an end time that he says will surely come. In verse 14 he writes: "For the earth will be filled with the knowledge of the glory of the Lord as the waters cover the sea." Notice that it is the *knowledge* of the glory of the Lord that this new messianic season will bring. Habakkuk understands that the earth is already full of God's glory. The challenge is not the absence of glory, but the absence of knowledge of the glory. In other words, the problem is not that God is somehow missing, but that His children are missing God. As the kingdom of God, launched with the resurrection of Jesus, comes into its fullness in the world, we are more and more able to find the glory of God even in the ordinary circumstances of our day-to-day lives. And when the kingdom of God comes in all its fullness, people will know the fullness of the glory of God in the same way that water fills the sea. That is pretty well completely!

Surprised by Glory

Sometimes God's glory surprises us, even in the darkest of places.

"Just give them some words of encouragement." The assignment from Rev. Michael Agwanda, director of Life for Children Ministries in Kenya, seemed simple enough. It was 9:30 p.m. and I was about to head out to meet with some of the thousand or so "street boys" of Kisumu . . . all homeless, penniless, and mostly forgotten. As we approached the first group, just

settling on the sidewalk for their night's rest, I found myself uncharacteristically at a loss for words.

What words would I have for abused, neglected, and abandoned boys of eleven, twelve, or thirteen? What comfort could I share with integrity? Their circumstances seemed so desperate, so hopeless. And the glory of God? I have to confess I was having a hard time seeing God's glory in this place. So, with no great words of wisdom coming to me, I prayed.

The Lord simply said, "Ask them their names." So, I did.

"My name is Godfrey," one boy said, with a soft, almost shy voice that belied his street-hardened countenance. It was not what I expected.

More unexpected, however, was the smile. It seemed almost out of place amidst the strong odor of unwashed bodies, the ragged clothing that had become a color one could only describe as "urban grime," the cracked and worn feet calloused by shoeless days, and the ubiquitous glue bottles. The challenges of daily life for these boys are hardly joy-inducing. Yet Godfrey lit up in a genuine smile, a smile that reached his eyes and brought light even in the darkness.

"My name is Godfrey," he said, and he smiled.

I don't know how long it had been since anyone had asked Godfrey his name. But he wanted me to know it. I asked him to tell me his story. I learned that his father was dead. His mother was a drug addict who had taken up with another man, also a drug addict. Both adults were physically abusive and neglectful, eventually throwing Godfrey out to fend for himself. And though his story is painful and difficult, he seemed to relish the opportunity to tell it. He had a story and it mattered to someone.

In the book of Job, we find a man who has become about as destitute as one can become. His family, wealth, health, and status have all been taken from him. As he suffers alone, scraping the sores on his body and wanting to die, some friends try to offer him some words of encouragement. After these men have failed over and over to give Job any real comfort, he finally implores them: "Listen carefully to my words; let this be the consolation that you give me" (Job 21:2). What he most wants is for someone to listen to his story with care; to hear him. To Job, this is the best (and perhaps only) consolation his friends can offer.

Although we had taken bread and milk out with us to share with the boys, I suspect that food was not what they really needed most. I believe Godfrey needed someone to ask his name, to hear his story, to help him continue to hope and believe that he mattered . . . to God and to other people. And by the grace of God, that need is one that every believer is capable of meeting in others. We need only be present, and in being present, share the presence of God in the lives of others.

As we prepared to leave, I asked the boys if I could get a picture with them so that I could remember them and their stories. I promised I would pray for them. They happily agreed to the photo. What I wasn't expecting was that just as the picture was being snapped, Godfrey would gently lay his head on my shoulder. Godfrey means "the peace of God," and that night, if only briefly, I believe the peace of God was present in that place. What I know for sure is that God's glory was there. I know because of what the seraphim say. But I also know because in that moment I saw the glory of God firsthand.

So often the greatest gift we can bring to others is to be the presence of the Father in their lives and know their names and their stories. Sometimes that is the very consolation the world needs. And it is often in those moments that the kingdom comes, and the knowledge of the glory of God fills the space, for us and for others.

The Focus of Our Gaze

And yet, despite the very real presence of God in every place, we often miss Him. Perhaps it is because so many times we put our focus on the wrong things. We focus on what is wrong, what is broken. We dwell on our challenges, our difficulties, what is missing, the weighty things of our lives. We forget that our Redeemer lives. We lose sight of the truth that "in all things God works for the good of those who love him, who have been called according to his purpose" (Rom. 8:28). Somewhere deep in our being we know that He will never leave us or forsake us, yet we forget that He is here!

This issue of focus is more important than we may realize. Indeed, science is teaching us how focus on the wrong things can cause us to miss even the most obvious realities taking place around us.

In the late 1990s, a pair of researchers named Christopher Chabris and Daniel Simons conducted a fascinating psychological experiment. The *New York Times* Sunday Book Review describes it this way: "It is one of the most famous psychological demos ever. Subjects are shown a video, about a minute long, of two teams, one in white shirts, the other in black shirts, moving around and passing basketballs to one another. They are asked to count the number of aerial and bounce passes made by the team wearing white, a seemingly simple task."[1] If you have never seen the video that is the centerpiece of this experiment, you might enjoy stopping right now, and taking the time to watch it online. Google "selective attention test" and simply follow the instructions on the video. The entire thing will only require eighty seconds.

For those who may not have been able to see the video, here is the fascinating part: at about the halfway mark, a woman wearing a black gorilla costume wanders right through the middle of the scene, stops briefly, and even pounds her chest while looking at the camera.

If you watched the video, did you see the gorilla? Typically, well more than half of people watching the video, when given the instruction to focus on the number of passes, will never see the gorilla. Yet, once people know the gorilla is there, it seems impossible to believe that anyone could miss it. As Simons and Chabris point out in their 2010 book entitled *The Invisible Gorilla*, human beings often don't see the most obvious things simply because other things have our attention and focus.

The Lamp of the Body

In Matthew 6:22–23 (again, the Sermon on the Mount) Jesus said something fascinating about our eyes: "The eye is the lamp of the body. If your eyes are healthy, your whole body will be full of light. But if your eyes are

---

1. Paul Bloom, "What We Miss," *New York Times* Sunday Book Review (June 6, 2010), 30.

unhealthy, your whole body will be full of darkness. If then the light within you is darkness, how great is that darkness!" This is a deep, multilayered teaching of our Lord. But among the many levels of meaning of this text, Jesus is again reminding us that *the focus of our gaze will determine the state of our being.* He is saying that if the focus of our eyes (and attention) is on the light (the glory of God), our whole being will be filled with light. But if our focus is always directed toward the darkness, our very souls become dark, our being weighed down with the heaviness of that darkness.

This is a profound truth, and it affects every area of our lives.

I know people who are constantly focused on evil, looking for the Devil in every situation. They are not evil themselves, but are preoccupied with the things of darkness. But if we spend our time looking for Satan, we are going to find him. If we are looking for what is wrong, or broken, or where our worries lie, we are going to see those things. And constant focus on the things of darkness only fills our lives, our souls, our beings, with darkness. Likewise, if we are looking for the face of God, if we are striving to see what Jesus is doing, we can remember again that Jesus Himself said, "Ask and it will be given to you; seek and you will find; knock and the door will be opened to you" (Matt. 7:7). When our focus is on the light and the glory of God, our very souls are filled with light. The light of God is present. Always. And when the time of uncertainty around the death of Uzziah came to Judah, when the whole nation was concerned, Isaiah saw the Lord seated on the throne, high and exalted, precisely because he was looking for the glory of God.

Where Is Our Focus?

So where do we focus our gaze? Warren Wiersbe, in his book *Be Distinct*, wrote: "when the outlook is bleak, try the uplook."[2] Though written many years ago, this remains good counsel today. Many of us need to adjust the focus of our gaze!

You may remember the old nursery rhyme "Pussycat, Pussycat" from your childhood:

> *Pussycat, pussycat where have you been?*
> *I've been to London to see the queen.*
> *Pussycat, pussycat, what saw you there?*
> *I saw a mouse run under the chair!*

What a silly little pussycat. Can you imagine? The cat goes off to London to see the queen. There, our feline seeker enters the throne room where the glory and the pomp and the beauty of the palace reside. And, in the center of it all, she encounters the queen in all her regal majesty. It is hard to conceive of anything that could overshadow all of that glory and wonder. It defies credulity to believe that anyone could miss the most glamorous things present in the room. But consider where the cat's focus lies. Not on the majesty, or the throne, or even the queen. Her focus is on

---

2. Warren Wiersbe, *Be Distinct: Standing Firmly Against the World's Tides* (OT Commentary 2 Kings and 2 Chronicles) (Colorado Springs, CO: David C. Cook, 2002), 184.

the floorboards, and the dust bunnies, and the mice running around under the chairs!

Can I tell you an unpleasant truth? We have a lot of pussycat Christians in the church. They come to church hoping to see the King of Glory, high and lifted up. And God is there. His glory is present. He wants to be seen. But many miss Him because they are too busy looking at the mice running around under the chairs.

"Did you see those stains on the carpet?"

"Did you notice what that woman was wearing this morning?"

"I don't like those hymns we sang today."

"The sound was too loud!"

"The preacher is boring."

"I'm just not being fed!"

We need to attend to our focus. We need to lift up our gaze!

The challenge posed by focusing on the wrong things is not limited to our worship experiences. As already stated, this truth will apply to every area of our lives: our relationships, our work, our family lives, even our enjoyment of our leisure activities. Over and over again I've witnessed how our focus determines what we see, which, in turn, determines how we experience our world and the people and circumstances in it.

Some of us have challenges with our children. For most parents, the arrival of a child in the family is a cause for celebration, wonder, and joy. I remember clearly staring into the trusting eyes of my firstborn as she was just hours old, considering the possibilities of her life and grateful that God had granted this miraculous blessing to us. But as our children grow, problems and frustrations emerge. There are seasons where we look at our children, these blessings from

God, and think, *These kids are going to drive me crazy!*
But these are the same creatures over whom we once
rejoiced—fearfully and wonderfully made, and still
endowed with the God-gifted life and potential they
possessed at their birth. So how do we so easily lose
sight of important realities in our children's lives? Do
we truly believe our children are a gift from God? Is
God involved in the mix?

I Can't Think of a Thing

Despite the passing of several decades, the memory is
as vivid as if it happened yesterday. During one of my
pastorates, a woman came to my office for counsel.

"I want to talk with you about my thirteen-year-
old son," she said. "He's driving me insane. He's just
awful. I'm seriously at a breaking point. I often think
I'd like to just send him away."

"Well, tell me about it," I said. And for the next hour
or so she poured out her soul. She really unloaded.
Disappointment, frustration, anger, and shame flowed
out of her as she described her son and his daily activities and way of being. By the time she was finished,
I had begun to sense that part of the problem was
the focus of her attention. When she started to wind
down, I asked if she had shared everything she was
concerned about.

"Yes," she replied with a sigh as a tear trickled
down her cheek.

"I simply have one question for you then," I said.
"What do you like about the boy?"

There was a long pause and she looked at the floor.
I had a watch on my desk, and I actually waited for
three minutes in silence while the question hung in

the air. That is a long time for silence in a situation like this one. Finally, she looked up at me with tears streaming down her face and said softly, "I can't think of a single thing."

"Okay, we've got two possibilities," I said. "Either you have given birth to the one truly and totally evil child on earth, and there is no good in him whatsoever—and I know the boy, so I know that isn't the case—or you have become so focused on what is wrong, on what you don't like about the boy, on your disappointments and anger with him, that you are no longer able to see the good that is in him. You can't see the gift of God that he is in your life. You can no longer see the light of life that is in him. What do you say we see if we can change the focus of your attention to what you actually love and enjoy about your son? What if we work to rediscover an understanding of how God is trying to bless your life through him? Because I assure you, the glory of God is here."

Of course, it was true that her son had some issues and there were challenges in their relationship. But the focus of her gaze was causing her to miss the glory of God and direct her constant attention to the broken parts of her son's life. In doing so, she was blind to so much of what was going on, and she was missing many of the blessings God was trying to sow into her life. The truth was her son actually had some wonderful, amazing qualities. He was really one of the nicest and best-behaved thirteen-year-olds in the church. And as his mother began to rediscover these things about her son, her feelings about him began to change dramatically.

Where is our focus? Are we looking for God? Do we believe that God is doing something, that His glory is present? Are we trying to seek out what God is up to?

The same concept applies to our marriage relationships. I had the opportunity to work with and be mentored by Pastor Wayne Cordeiro in Hawaii. Prior to this season, in the earlier years of my ministry, I used to ask couples getting married if they loved each other. Pastor Wayne suggested to me that this was a self-evident question. It seems very unlikely that two people would present themselves for marriage if they didn't already believe that they loved each other. Instead, Pastor Wayne suggested: "Ask them if, in this moment, they truly believe that God has placed this woman or this man in their lives in order to be their life mate? Is it God who is bringing this relationship together?"

Let's be honest, if you have been married for fifteen minutes you know that there are times when you are so grateful to God for putting this amazing person in your life, but there are also times when you look across the room and think, *God couldn't have meant that!* It is in these moments of doubt and irritation that you have to know in your heart that God played a role in bringing the two of you together. When we remember that God is involved in the relationship, and that God is doing something, we can put our focus on what God is doing. We can mentally assent to the idea that God knew what He was doing, and that if God did this, He did it for our good! There is a line at the end of the marriage blessing that says, "Those whom God has brought together, let no human being tear asunder." When we ignore what God is doing in our relationships, we run the risk of destroying a spiritual unity that God intended for our good. But sometimes remembering the promise of God in our marriages gets lost in our focus on the problems and challenges.

I will never forget the morning I came to my office at New Hope after a little spat that had occurred with my wife the evening before. (Yes, pastors have marital spats like everyone else.) I came into work looking like someone had stolen my little red wagon!

Pastor Wayne looked at me and said, "What in the world is wrong with you?

"Oh, Pastor Wayne," I said, "it is this woman that God has put in my life . . . she's driving me crazy!"

He chuckled and said, "Are you listening to yourself? Did you hear what you just said? Do you really believe God put her in your life?"

"Well, yes, Pastor Wayne, but—"

He interrupted my protests: "Well, did God just decide to mess with you? Did God wake up one day and say, 'Hey angels, watch this: I'm going to mess with Max. I have someone really special for everyone else, but I have a real loser for this guy. I'm going to make him miserable'?"

Pastor Wayne continued: "You go home and cherish that woman. Because God knew exactly what He was doing when He put Anna in my life, and He knew what He was doing when He put Dee Dee in yours. Her name is Dorothy. You know the Greek: *Doros,* meaning 'gift,' and *theos,* meaning 'God.' The gift of God. Try not to forget that. And if you seem to lose sight of it when you start to focus on what you don't like, remind yourself of who put her in your life in the first place."

I have never forgotten. And while there are, of course, times when I don't live up to my commitment to love, honor, and cherish Dee Dee (the "gift of God"), and there are too many times when I need to remind myself, there are also many wonderful moments when I can focus on what God is doing in our marriage, and I can see the glory. In those moments my relationship and my being are brought into the light. It is truly all about the focus.

When we can move our attention away from the challenges, difficulties, disappointments, and frustrations with our relationships, and instead try to focus on discovering where God is, and where His glory is present in these relationships, we can move from brokenness to gratitude and blessing. In all of these things there are lessons for us to learn. There are ways that God is at work, molding and shaping our character. But we forget sometimes that God is not just seated on the throne, high and exalted. He is also as close as the very air that we breathe, and His glory fills the whole earth. The Lord is with us and pulling for us, and He's there to be found if we lift up our gaze and seek Him.

Think about These Things

The church at Philippi was one of the apostle Paul's favorite churches. Founded in the midst of intense persecution and adversity, this church brought Paul great joy. So much so, that when he wrote his letter to them, he said:

> I thank my God every time I remember you. In all my prayers for all of you, I always pray with joy because of your partnership in the gospel from the first day until now, being confident of this, that he who began a good work in you

will carry it on to completion until the day of
Christ Jesus. (Phil. 1:3–6)

I'm absolutely certain the church in Philippi had
problems. I'm sure not everything was praiseworthy.
And no doubt Paul could have found much about
which to complain. But note the positivity in Paul's
statement. He's thankful "every time," in "all my
prayers," for "all of you," and he always prayed "with
joy." How can he say these things? Precisely because
he believes the Lord began something in Philippi and
is still working and able to bring it to completion. Paul
knows the glory of the Lord is present with the people
of the church. And because Paul chooses to focus his
attention on what God is doing in and through them,
he is able to rejoice. And Paul doesn't want the people
of Philippi (or us) to miss this point. Thus, he comes to
the end of this same brilliant letter by writing:

> Finally, brothers and sisters, whatever is true,
> whatever is noble, whatever is right, what-
> ever is pure, whatever is lovely, whatever is
> admirable—if anything is excellent or praise-
> worthy—think about such things. (Phil. 4:8)

Paul's counsel to the Philippian church is still
valid today. And it is far more than the power of positive thinking. It is not just thinking happy thoughts or
whistling in the dark. And it certainly is not burying
our collective heads in the sand and denying the reality
of problems and trials in a broken and hurting world.
Instead, it is an acknowledgment that the seraphim
got it right: the whole earth *is* full of the glory of God.
We think about the truth because truth is still to be
found all around us. Jesus said, "I am the truth" (see

John 14:6), and He has promised to be with us always (see Matthew 28:20). The same is true of nobility, righteousness, purity, and loveliness. We need only ask the Lord for eyes to see them. And while any five-year-old can walk into a room and point out what is wrong, or broken, or bad, it takes a mature spirit to search for and focus on what is excellent and praiseworthy.

"To be, or not to be," Prince Hamlet utters in perhaps Shakespeare's most famous line, "that is the question." In the spiritual life, however, a far more important question is: To see, or not to see? As we will discover, what we see can greatly affect our spiritual lives and our being. And what we seek, what we pay attention to, will largely determine what we see.

TWO

Becoming a Grace Hunter

When he arrived and saw what the grace of God had done, he was glad and encouraged them all to remain true to the Lord with all their hearts.

—ACTS 11:23

Let's be honest: even when we believe that the glory of God fills the whole earth, our lives can still be quite dark at times. Sometimes the darkness becomes so heavy, the problems so challenging, the circumstances so discouraging that it can be hard to find any light at all. It is one thing to believe that God's glory is always present, but quite another to know how and where to find it.

I was right in the middle of the forest trail when my flashlight failed. It was well past midnight and the simple pathway wound through a densely wooded area. Suddenly surrounded by a darkness as thick as any I had ever experienced, I was afraid.

As a young adult, I was involved with leading
a rustic summer camp for middle-school children.
This church camp, located on 660 acres of unde-
veloped woodlands along the bank of the Suwanee
River in Florida, afforded the youth a true wilderness experience. A few scattered cinder block cabins
with no electricity, four or five fire pits for open-air
cooking, and a "head shed" with the only electric
lights and refrigerators made up the only manmade
improvements in an otherwise pristine forest. A series
of long, twisting trails connected the various cabins
and activity centers of the camp. Over the years I had
grown to know these trails like the back of my hand,
having walked them all countless times. I felt right at
home in this camp.

The whole thing had really been a bad idea from
the start. On the night in question, my late adolescent
brain had decided it would be fun to play a prank on
one of my buddies. He had a group of campers in a
distant cabin. I planned to slip up close to his cabin, sit
in the darkness, and make some wild animal noises to
see what kind of a reaction I could get out of his crew.
Assuredly, this was not the most mature or responsible
thing for a camp counselor to do. It would not matter;
I would never make it to their cabin anyway. I was
about halfway there when my flashlight flickered and
went dead. Suddenly, the familiar trail disappeared
as my world became pitch black. The animal noises I
heard (or imagined) were not the result of some juvenile counselor playing a prank, but instead the bobcats
and screech owls and other creatures of the night who
made those woods their home. As I stood still in that
darkness, I was not sure how to proceed. I began to

think the only solution was to sit down right where I was and wait for sunrise. But even as that depressing thought occurred to me, something nearby rustled in the leaves and I began to imagine all manner of unpleasant things that could turn up as I sat on that trail. I needed a different plan.

I'm sad to admit that it took me, a church camp leader and budding pastor, a few minutes to consider that now might be a good time for prayer! But under the circumstances, rather than kneeling and bowing my head in prayer, I chose to look up to the heavens and, with eyes open, let my "requests be made known to God" (Phil. 4:6 HCSB). It was a simple prayer, really; something along the lines of: "HELP!" (As an aside, that is often the most sincere and effective prayer a believer can pray!)

As I was praying, I became aware that I could see the stars. Beautiful stars. And although the idea of seeing stars in the sky might not seem surprising given that it was the middle of the night, it suddenly dawned on me that it isn't normally possible to see the stars in the forest. The tree canopy tends to block the light. I realized that the only reason I could see the stars was because I was on the path which created a slight opening in the tree cover. With this new discovery in mind, I determined that if I simply walked very slowly and carefully while looking up, I could determine when I was on the correct path by keeping my eyes on the heavens. If I could see the starlight clearly, I was almost certainly on the path. And if I lost sight of the stars, it meant I had moved off the path and needed to make an adjustment. It took quite a long time to cover the distance that night. Yet, by keeping my eyes on the tiny bit of light the heavens provided, I was able to stay on the pathway to my cabin, and the security and safety that cabin would provide.

I learned several lessons that evening. But the most important and significant one has great spiritual implications: when your light fails, look up!

Not many are likely to find themselves alone on a forest trail in the middle of the night without a flashlight. But nearly all of us will experience periods of darkness and uncertainty in our lives spiritually, emotionally, and relationally. In a very real sense, the same thing that got me safely off of that trail so many years ago can serve us well in all of the dark places of our lives: Look up! Look for the light of God.

Isaiah not only understood this reality, he also tried to prepare the world for it. During the darkest period of the exile of God's people, Isaiah told them of a day when the light would come into the world: "The people walking in darkness have seen a great light; on those living in the land of deep darkness a light has dawned" (Isa. 9:2). Isaiah foresaw the coming of the Light of the World, our Lord Jesus.

The apostle John later declared about the coming of Jesus: "The light shines in the darkness, and the darkness has not overcome it" (John 1:5). Of course, John is not trying to deny the presence of darkness in our lives, nor is he trying to downplay the challenges and significance of that darkness. He is, however, reminding us that there is no darkness deep enough to overcome the light. And the Light has come into the world to stay!

That is why the apostle Peter sought to encourage the persecuted, beleaguered, and increasingly discouraged early church disciples with these words: "But you are a chosen people, a royal priesthood, a holy nation, God's special possession, that you may declare the praises of him who called you out of darkness into his wonderful light" (1 Peter 2:9). Light can often give us the courage we need in dark situations. And, as Peter well understood, there are times in our lives when we can all use some encouragement.

The Son of Encouragement

I want to be Barnabas when I grow up!

This is a man whose name only appears a few times in the New Testament, and then often in the background. He is certainly not as well-known as Peter, Paul, John, or even young Timothy. We don't have any records of his sermons. He left no confirmed writings. He was not an apostle. Yet the fingerprints of this wonderful saint are all over the early church. His influence is remarkable.

Born to a devout Levite family from the Mediterranean island of Cyprus, he was given the name Joseph by his parents. At some point in his childhood the family moved from Cyprus to Jerusalem, where the young Joseph was educated in the traditions of Rabbinical Judaism. Many believe that he was a student of the great rabbi Gamaliel, along with a young Saul. Although it is unknown exactly when or how Joseph met and became a follower of Jesus, we know that he was numbered among the earliest disciples. As an adult he was also a person of means who owned property and had a large family in and around Jerusalem.

It wasn't until Joseph committed an act of great generosity and devotion to the Lord that he was first called Barnabas. The early church was suffering. The original disciples had largely been poor, working-class men. They had followed Jesus for more than three years, depending largely on hospitality and the gifts of some of the women who followed Jesus for their sustenance. Most of these young disciples had no formal education. They were not part of the establishment of Jerusalem. Following Pentecost, when the church grew rapidly under the power of the Holy Spirit and the bold preaching and witness of these same disciples, an intense persecution arose and the impoverished early church leaders who stayed in Jerusalem were driven deep into the shadows. According to the book of Acts, the believers in this early church community pooled and shared all they had, and as a result there were no needy among them (see Acts 4:32–35). Nevertheless, finances were tight and times were hard.

Joseph, sensing the need and prompted by the Holy Spirit, sold a piece of property he owned and brought the money to the apostles, giving it generously to them for the use of the community of believers. It was at this time that the disciples began to call him Barnabas, which Luke tells us means "son of encouragement" (see Acts 4:36–37).

The great Scottish poet Robert Burns, in one of his most famous lines, exclaims: "O wad some Power the giftie gie us, to see oursels as ithers see us!"[1] A more current translation would be something along the lines of: "Oh would some Power the gift give us, to see ourselves as others see us." What a wonderful gift the early church gave to Barnabas in giving him

1. Robert Burns, "To a Louse," *Burns: Everyman's Library Pocket Poets* (New York: Alfred A. Knopf, 2006), 9.

this descriptive name. It captured the essence of how others saw him, and the treasure he was to the church.

Bar-Nabbas, the son of *"nabbas"* in Hebrew, is rendered by Luke in Greek as *"huios paraklesis."* Luke translates *"paraklesis"* as "encouragement," thus making Barnabas mean "son of encouragement." *Paraklesis*, however, can also mean exhortation and consolation (or comfort). Thus, Barnabas can mean "son of encouragement," "son of comfort and consolation," or even "son of exhortation." And it was truly all three of these qualities that the people of the early church saw in Barnabas. He was an encourager, a comforter, and an exhorter. We will see how these character traits played out in Barnabas's life, and why this was such a richly deserved honorific for him.

The Greek word *paraklesis* is also related to the Greek descriptive *Paraclete*, one of the names Jesus uses for the Holy Spirit. Jesus indicates that when the Holy Spirit comes, He will come alongside believers to encourage, comfort, and exhort them. It is no surprise, therefore, that the book of Acts says of Barnabas: "He was a good man, full of the Holy Spirit and faith" (Acts 11:24a). The infilling of the Holy Spirit caused Barnabas to seek the Lord in faith, and to become a man of encouragement, comfort, and exhortation as the Spirit worked in and through him. It is hard to overstate the impact Barnabas's life had on the church and the people of his day.

Grace Hunter

Perhaps the best example of Barnabas the Encourager is found in his interactions with the Gentile believers in Antioch. It was in this, the third largest city in the Roman Empire, that a small sect within the Jewish world broke out to become the Christian faith that would transform the world. And Barnabas was right in the middle of it, playing a central role.

When persecution of the followers of Jesus erupted in Jerusalem following the stoning death of Stephen, believers were scattered to the various parts of the Roman Empire and beyond. Although Jesus told the disciples that they would be His witnesses "in Jerusalem, and in all Judea and Samaria, and to the ends of the earth" (Acts 1:8), they had largely remained in Jerusalem prior to the persecution. Even with this scattering of the disciples, most of the witnessing was taking place among members of the Jewish diaspora in the various places the disciples landed. It wasn't long, however, before non-Jewish residents in these lands began to hear and respond to the message of the early evangelists. Soon word got to Jerusalem that a group of Gentile (non-Jewish) people was worshiping together in Antioch and claiming to be followers of Jesus. Luke writes: "News of this reached the church in Jerusalem, and they sent Barnabas to Antioch" (Acts 11:22).

The church in Jerusalem was made up of devout lifelong Jewish believers. Although they were undergoing persecution within the Jewish community, they still considered themselves faithful Hebrews. The news of Gentile followers of Jesus would have come to them as a surprise and somewhat of a shock. Could it be that God planned to include the Gentiles in this good news? Even in young communities and institutions, change is often hard to accept and embrace. The early church was no exception. When the scripture says, "they sent

Barnabas to Antioch," there can be little question that they meant for him to discover what these believers in Antioch were doing wrong and put a stop to it. This thing seemed to be getting out of hand!

If James and Peter and the other early leaders of the church in Jerusalem wanted to put God in a box, or to figure out how to derail the exciting things God was doing through the Holy Spirit, they picked the wrong man to send on that mission. From the outset, the Son of Encouragement went in looking for God, looking for God's glory, and looking to encourage what God was doing. I love what the next verse says: "When he arrived and saw what the grace of God had done, he was glad and encouraged them all to remain true to the Lord with all their hearts" (Acts 11:23). Let's look closely at this powerful announcement.

First, Luke says, he "saw what the grace of God had done." I imagine the leaders of the church in Jerusalem sent Barnabas with instructions to determine what this group of Gentiles in Antioch might be doing wrong. So often that is the case in life. As human beings, we find it easy to find fault. We state our objections, notice shortcomings and failings, and look for what is wrong. And, as we saw in the last chapter, we always tend to find what we are seeking and notice what we are looking for.

Barnabas, however, was a grace hunter! He showed up in Antioch already convinced that God was up to something, and excitedly ready to discover exactly what that something was. The scripture says that when he arrived, he "saw what the grace of God had done." Why was it the grace of God that Barnabas saw? Because that is what he was looking for. As with Isaiah, Barnabas seemed obviously to believe that God's glory filled the earth. He believed that, in Jesus Christ, the grace of God was breaking out all over the place, in wildly unexpected ways. He didn't turn up in Antioch expecting to find problems to fix or things he needed to shut down. Undoubtedly there were problems that needed to be fixed, and some practices that were out of line with the newfound faith of the believers in Antioch. These things could be and would be addressed down the line. But all of those things paled in comparison to the wonders of God's grace, operative and life-giving, being demonstrated in the faith community of Antioch. Barnabas saw the grace of God and what that grace was doing in Antioch precisely because that is exactly what he expected to see and what he was looking for in the first place. This grace-hunter approach was Barnabas's default orientation to the world, brought about by the Holy Spirit operating in his life.

Second, Luke says Barnabas "was glad" (Acts 11:23). The actual words of Luke are a bit stronger. He literally says that Barnabas rejoiced greatly, in the sense of being filled with strong emotions of gladness. Barnabas didn't casually shrug it off, thinking, *Well, this is nice.* The text basically tells us that he was ecstatic, filled with joy, and celebrating not just the wonderful things God was doing among the Gentiles at Antioch, but the fact that he was able to experience and be a part of it all. Barnabas was a grace hunter, and when he found what he was looking for, it made his heart soar.

I was talking about a friend of mine one day some years ago, when that very friend walked into the room. I looked up and just casually said, "Speak of the Devil . . .". Without missing a beat, my friend replied, "Well, I guess you should always speak of the one you know best!" It was a playful conversation among friends, and no one was upset. But later that evening I thought about my friend's reply. Even though both he and I were being flippant, he was onto something in what he said. Too many people are focused on the things of the Enemy. It is possible to spend our time so focused on these things that, in the end, they become what we know best. When the expectation of finding the things of the Enemy becomes our norm, we tend to only see those things. And it is hard to get much joy and happiness out of a mindset filled with thoughts of evil, even if we believe we are in opposition to that evil.

Barnabas was confident that the grace of God was operative in the world. He was convinced he would find the grace of God operative in Antioch. And he understood that when he found what he was looking for, joy would be the result, and that joy would be contagious.

Finally, Luke tells us that in addition to rejoicing over what he discovered in Antioch, Barnabas "encouraged them all" (Acts 11:23). Any fears these Gentiles had that the great Jewish leader from Jerusalem might be coming to shut down their work and ministry, or to put binders and restrictions on them, were quickly dispelled. Quite the contrary, Barnabas built the people up, pointed out the amazing things he saw among them, and then came alongside them (for a year!) to join in what God was doing in their community. As a result, "a great number of people were brought to the Lord" (v. 24), and the church continued to grow and flourish. In fact, it was at this point that the followers of Jesus were first called "Christians" or "little Christs" (v. 26). Son of Encouragement, indeed!

A Call for Us All

The world needs more grace hunters! Plain and simple. In a world that seems to be increasingly antagonistic, where dissatisfaction and depression, even despair, are growing at alarming rates, society needs women and men who know that the grace of God is still alive and operative. We need people who can not only seek and find that grace, and the glory of God it reveals, but also help the world to see it and celebrate along with them. If you have ever met a Spirit-filled grace hunter, you understand just how wonderful they can be and why we need them.

I am grateful to my dear friend João Carlos Lopes, a longtime pastor and bishop in the Methodist Church of Brazil, for helping me to see this grace-hunting character in Barnabas. It was Bishop Lopes who first pointed out to me what was really going on in this passage of Scripture. But even more important, Bishop Lopes has shown me how this same grace-hunting approach to life and ministry can be lived out today.

More than twenty years ago, just a few months after his fortieth birthday, João Carlos was elected to the episcopacy in Brazil. As a strong pastor from a humble background, the newly elected bishop was sent to the sixth ecclesiastical region of the Brazilian Methodist Church, an area in the south of the country that was not known as a stronghold of the church. Indeed, it was considered by many at the time to be a backwater, and getting assigned there was not looked upon as a great opportunity. Bishop Lopes knew, however, that the grace of God was operative in his region, and he knew that the people there could experience that grace with great joy if he could open them up to it and encourage them to grow in it.

Where others saw the crime and desperate poverty that existed in the favelas in his area, João Carlos saw God at work in the hearts and lives of beaten down believers in these same communities and began to empower them to plant and grow life-giving churches right where they were. Where others saw rural communities seemingly left behind by urbanization and the technologically driven modern economy, João Carlos saw God at work in life-giving faith communities that could become the lifeblood of those very towns and regions. While others were wringing their hands over the secularization and materialism of the growing cities in the south, João Carlos saw opportunities for increasing numbers of women and men to find meaning and purpose in the growing communities of faith in these same cities. He celebrated, with great joy, the grace of God that was already operative in the lives of the people of his region, and he came alongside these same people, encouraging them, and giving them opportunities to live into their calling to join Jesus in His gracious work in their lives and communities.

Over the two decades since his election, Bishop Lopes has seen the sixth region transformed. I had the privilege of visiting many of the communities in his area a few years ago. Everywhere we went, I discovered groups of enthusiastic followers of Jesus joyously celebrating what God was doing among them and filled with vision for what God could and would do going forward. The joy was contagious. And the recognition that God's grace was flowing in their midst and all around them was undeniable. João Carlos Lopes had come into their lives as a grace hunter. His ministry among them, in the power of the Holy Spirit, had encouraged thousands of men and women to recognize and celebrate that grace, and to embrace it in their own lives. It was a beautiful and encouraging thing to behold. May the grace-hunter tribe increase and multiply, to the glory of God.

The Son of Exhortation

"Young man, I don't want to frighten you, but God told me to tell you something." The elderly man had gently grasped my shoulder as I walked down the aisle after a Sunday evening worship service. I was fifteen years old and visiting the church with a friend from high school who attended there. I had never attended this church before and had never met the serious and somewhat severe-looking gentleman who was speaking to me. But I did recognize him from the worship service that had just ended.

Earlier in the service, the pastor mentioned a young girl in the congregation who was having some hearing problems. He said they were going to have healing prayer and called on someone by name to come forward and pray over the little girl for God's healing. The man who would later speak to me slowly made his way forward. I had never seen healing prayer done in a church service and I was fascinated to experience what would happen next. The old man stood behind the little girl at the front of the church, placed his hands gently over her ears, and with a sonorous voice began to pray. Everyone else had their heads bowed in reverent prayer. I, however, was staring wide-eyed at the old man. I wanted to see what would happen. Much to my surprise, while he never stopped praying, he kept his eyes open as well—and was staring straight back at me! Then, almost as soon as it had begun, the prayer was over. Nothing extraordinary happened, and I do not know to this day whether the young girl was healed. The elderly gentleman returned to his seat, and the service continued.

Now, this same man had approached me from behind, grasping my shoulder as he delivered his message: "The Lord told me to tell you that you are to preach His Word, and that you will be a powerful preacher if you will answer the call." My adolescent brain had no idea how to respond to this strange man I had just met. Not only had no one ever said anything like that to me before, no one in the church I regularly attended with my family ever said or did things like this man. "I'm just delivering the message," the man continued. "What you do with it now is between you and the Lord."

My friend who had invited me to the service that evening saw the look of confusion on my face and pulled me away toward the door. As we walked outside, he whispered to me, "Don't worry about him. He's just a harmless old man. He won't bother you." We went on to whatever teenaged antics we were about in those days and I didn't give the old man and his words much more thought . . . until some years later, when I began to wrestle with the idea that I might really have a pastoral calling on my life. And I wondered about the words of exhortation the stranger had shared with me, the words he said the Lord told him to share.

Exhortation is about urging or persuasively encouraging someone to do something, typically something of importance or significance. And for people who are aware that the glory of the Lord fills the whole earth, they often see what God is doing not just in situations or circumstances, but also in the lives of other people. For these people, exhortation is about helping others understand and live into what God is doing in their lives. And Barnabas was definitely one of these people.

Saul of Tarsus was a devastating figure in the life of the early church. A Pharisee who had studied the Law under the great Jewish rabbi Gamaliel, Saul was a fierce opponent of all followers of Jesus. And after witnessing with great approval the martyrdom of Stephen, Saul had become a great persecutor of the church. Under orders from the high priest, he was seeking out followers of Jesus both inside and outside Israel, imprisoning them or having them executed. To the members of the fledgling church in Jerusalem, he was one of the most feared men alive.

The story of Saul's encounter with Jesus on the road to Damascus, and his subsequent decision to become a disciple and take up the cause of Jesus, is one of the most powerful stories in church history. But it was one thing for Saul to follow Jesus in Damascus, it was quite another for him to have fellowship with the church in Jerusalem, among the very people he had been persecuting. Once again, Barnabas saves the day:

> When he [Saul] came to Jerusalem, he tried to join the disciples, but they were all afraid of him, not believing that he really was a disciple. But Barnabas took him and brought him to

the apostles. He told them how Saul on his journey had seen the Lord and that the Lord had spoken to him, and how in Damascus he had preached fearlessly in the name of Jesus. (Acts 9:26–27)

Imagine the courage this act took for Barnabas. Saul was not just someone who had spoken harshly about believers. He was responsible for the suffering and deaths of many followers of Jesus, including family and friends of the apostles and early church leaders. The disciples in the Jerusalem church were justified in their fear of Saul. When they saw him, they were intimately aware of his faults and failures, and had good reason to be suspicious of his motives.

Barnabas, on the other hand, once again demonstrates an amazing capacity for seeing beyond the obvious problems and evil in the situation. It isn't that he is unaware of who Saul is or what he represents. But Barnabas is also able to see deeper, into what God is trying to do. He believes in the transformative power of God's grace. He believes that the Lord can redeem people and use them for His greater purposes. And because of his faith and the prompting of the Holy Spirit, he is willing to put his own reputation on the line, and his life as well, in order to bring Saul into the community of faith. Based on Barnabas's word, Saul is received by the church in Jerusalem, and later sent back home to Tarsus, where he grows in faith and discipleship.

Nearly everyone knows and understands how important the apostle Paul was for the early church and the expansion of the church into Asia and Europe. But without the exhortation ministry of Barnabas,

Paul's ministry and all that the Lord wanted to do in and through Paul might have died before it could even get started.

The Son of Comfort and Consolation

If we live long enough, and attempt to do anything challenging with our lives, all of us will eventually experience disappointment and failure. These things go hand in hand with life. What often makes a lasting difference in our lives during these moments of failure is the response of the people around us.

I was barely eighteen years old when I prepared to run my first physical fitness test in the military. I was in an officers' training program at Vanderbilt University, and though I was already sworn into the program, it was still necessary to pass the PFT. That included running three miles in a certain time. On the day of the test, I was nowhere near properly prepared.

Training would have been the sensible way to get ready for this event. But I really disliked running at that age, and I had developed a lot of bad habits that were inconsistent with athletic training. So, I just decided to wing it. I assumed I could just run as hard and fast as possible and gut it out until the end. It didn't help that I had stayed out late the night before eating and drinking with friends with reckless abandon. I was already queasy with both anxiety and an upset stomach when we began the three-mile run.

I took off like a shot and ran with the fastest runners for the first quarter mile or so, after which I was completely spent. To add insult to injury, my stomach rebelled, and I ended up in the bushes beside the trail quite sick. As I knelt there in embarrassment and defeat, trying not to be noticed by anyone, I sensed someone towering over me. I looked up into the eyes of our unit's commanding officer, Capt. Sidney Banks, USN. Although he was well into his fifties, and was no longer required to run the PFT, Captain Banks always suited up and ran with us anyway. He was that kind of guy. Only, at this moment, he had stopped running and was peering down at me with great concern. "Are you going to be okay, Midshipman Wilkins?" he asked, surprising me that he even knew my name. "I think so, sir," I replied, but with not much enthusiasm. Captain Banks knelt beside me and placed his hand on my shoulder. "Young man, do you think you can get up and try to finish if I run along with you to encourage you?" What could I say? There was no way I could turn him down.

The two of us ran along, very slowly at first, until the nausea began to pass, then we picked up the pace a bit, with the captain whispering encouragement to me every couple of minutes. As we passed the two-and-a-half-mile mark, he said to me, "Midshipman, don't you think you should run on ahead of me now, and finish strong? It might not look too good to the others if you come running in with the old man!" I'm not really sure where I found the wherewithal to bolt ahead of him and get across the finish line, but I did, and then collapsed on the ground. I had completed the run with eleven seconds to spare, and I passed the test.

Following the run, however, I fully expected to be berated by my superiors, including Captain Banks, for my sad performance. I had done everything wrong: I'd failed to train, I had ignored the counsel to eat well and get a good night's rest the evening before, and I had ignored all instruction about pacing myself. In fact, the only reason I had finished at all was because I was ashamed to stay in the shrubs on my knees while the captain encouraged me to get going. I was disappointed in myself and wondering if I even belonged in this elite military unit.

Then Captain Banks spoke. He gathered our entire unit together and began by saying, "I saw something today that inspired me. It made me proud to be a part of this unit. I found Midshipman Wilkins sick beside the trail. But while a lesser man would have stayed down, he found the intestinal fortitude to get up and run through the pain. He finished the race. He showed me something. It takes character to run through a 'sick' and I couldn't be prouder of that midshipman right now. Let's congratulate him." And the entire unit dutifully applauded.

I learned something about extraordinary leadership that day. I know that I had done nothing worthy of praise. I know that Captain Banks knew why I was sick, and that there was nothing particularly praiseworthy in my performance. He also knew that the others in the unit were already looking at me with derision and even contempt. Everyone else had finished before I did. But the captain also knew that while people can easily be defined by their failures, it doesn't have to be that way. From the moment he encountered me in that hedgerow, he sought to comfort me, to console me, and to come alongside me to build me back up and get me home. Then he had the compassion and wisdom to turn my failure into an opportunity for growth, by pointing out the only positive he could have found in the whole mess in order to encourage me. It not only had its intended effect, but I also determined then and there that I would do whatever I could to never let Captain Banks down again. I wanted to become the person he was telling everyone else I was. And while I know that he knew I was not really that person at the time, I think that he truly believed I could become that man.

Those with a spirit of comfort and consolation can make a lasting difference in the lives of others during times of disappointment and failure. And Barnabas had just such a spirit.

The First Missionary Journey

The church at Antioch was growing numerically and spiritually. The disciples decided, after much prayer, to send forth missionaries to share the good news of the kingdom in other Roman towns and provinces. Barnabas and Paul were selected for the journey and, after a prayerful commissioning, they were sent on their way.

Having made their way to Jerusalem, Paul and Barnabas were preparing to leave for other parts when a respected young man named John Mark agreed to accompany them as a helper. Most likely a youth at the time, he was from a wealthy family of disciples. The prospect of having him along for the journey must have gladdened the hearts of the two missionaries. They headed off to the island of Cypress, and then to Asia Minor.

I like to imagine the conversation between these three men as they journeyed. I assume Paul and Barnabas must have regaled John Mark with tales of the miraculous power of God and the outpouring of the Holy Spirit throughout their journey. I suspect that the stories of life transformations along the way were exciting and compelling. But I assume that the two wizened missionaries also shared with their young assistant the realities of the persecutions, the deprivation, the dangers, and the disappointments inherent in a missionary journey. Whatever the case, although the Bible doesn't say exactly why, upon reaching Pamphylia (well before the end of the trip), John Mark left and went home. It was a disappointing end to a promising beginning.

Paul and Barnabas successfully completed their journey without John Mark. They returned to Antioch and celebrated all the wonders the Lord had performed during their trip, and the people rejoiced. Then, in Acts 15 we read:

> Some time later Paul said to Barnabas, "Let us go back and visit the believers in all the towns where we preached the word of the Lord and see how they are doing." Barnabas wanted to take John, also called Mark, with them, but Paul did not think it wise to take him, because he had deserted them in Pamphylia and had not continued with them in the work. (vv. 36–38)

It is clear that Paul considered John Mark's abandonment of the mission as a disqualifying failure. The idea of taking the youth along on another journey apparently infuriated Paul. So much so, that he and Barnabas had a sharp disagreement over John Mark's participation and ended up parting ways. Paul selected Silas and went off one way, while Barnabas picked up John Mark and headed off another. I don't think this episode represents Paul's finest hour, but we can certainly see Barnabas's spirit of comfort and consolation on full display.

Yes, John Mark had let down the team on the first missionary journey. He was young and probably ill-prepared the first time out. But Barnabas did not want to see his early failure define the young man's future. Like Captain Banks during my first PFT, Barnabas picked up the downcast John Mark and encouraged him to get back on the right path and finish the race. And the church of Jesus Christ is forever in his debt for this magnanimous act of consolation.

During those early days of the church everyone was expecting the imminent return of Jesus. No one thought to write down the story of Jesus' life and ministry. Why bother when He would be returning any day? But as time passed and the Lord's return seemed delayed, one young man—a close companion of both Peter and Barnabas—was inspired by the Holy Spirit to write the entire story. Later, both Luke and Matthew, and then even the great apostle John would be similarly inspired. But scholars agree that the first of the gospel writers was that same reticent missionary, John Mark, who, under the inspiration of the Spirit, gave us the gospel of Mark.

Think of it: without John Mark the world may never have had a written gospel of Jesus. And if it had not been for Barnabas, the Son of Consolation, who picked him up at one of his lowest moments, John Mark may never have lived into his calling. We know from his later letters that Paul was eventually reconciled with John Mark, and that John Mark went on to be one of the great saints and leaders in the church. The impact of a few well-placed words of consolation and comfort had made all the difference, and likely changed the course of history.

Encourage One Another

While no one knows for sure who wrote the book of Hebrews in the New Testament, there are some scholars who suspect it may have been Barnabas. There is no indication in the book of who authored it, which somehow seems fitting to the behind-the-scenes character of Barnabas the Encourager. Whether or not he wrote the book, however, there are some sentiments in Hebrews that certainly align with who Barnabas was. Among those passages is this treasure:

> And let us consider how we may spur one another on toward love and good deeds, not giving up meeting together, as some are in the habit of doing, but encouraging one another—and all the more as you see the Day approaching. (Heb. 10:24–25)

The world needs more grace hunters. We would benefit from more people who know that the glory of God fills the whole earth, who believe that God is at work in the world and in the lives of every person they meet, and who seek to "spur one another on toward love and good deeds." And as dark and overwhelming as the world can be at times, as discouraging as our fears and failures may seem, and as we "see the Day approaching," we might all consider how we could encourage one another. Barnabas certainly lived out these words. God knows we could use more like him.

THREE

The Inward Look

> *"Woe to me!" I cried. "I am ruined! For I am a man of unclean lips, and I live among a people of unclean lips, and my eyes have seen the King, the LORD Almighty."*
>
> —ISAIAH 6:5

Have you ever seen a bull moose hiding behind a tree?

Although I had heard stories about the hiding habits of moose for years, I was still amused when I saw it in person for the first time. I was visiting Rocky Mountain National Park when I came across three people standing still and staring into the forest. I quietly stepped over to see what they were looking at and there he was: a full-grown bull moose, probably weighing around a thousand pounds, with his nose pressed up against a slender aspen tree. He was standing completely still, apparently convinced he was hidden from the small crowd of camera-laden tourists.

It was a comical scene: a big, broad belly sticking out
on both sides of the tree, antlers appearing to grow out
of the tree's bark, and four skinny moose legs to round
out the scene. I had to laugh. With his narrow-set eyes
pressed up against the trunk of the tree, the moose
could not see us, and thus, he was convinced that we
could not see him. He was hiding in plain sight, but the
only one really fooled was the moose.

I think of that moose often when I consider how
human beings, with all of our gifts of reason and
intellect, are still able to convince ourselves that we
can hide from our creator God. From the moment in
the garden of Eden when Adam and Eve tasted the
forbidden fruit and sin made its horrific entry into the
created order, the human response to knowledge of
our failures and shortcomings has been to try to hide
from God. It is no less ridiculous for a human being to
think himself or herself capable of hiding from God
than for a bull moose to believe it can hide behind an
aspen. Yet, the fact this behavior is preposterous has
not prevented every generation of human beings from
trying to do so.

God is not deceived by our hiding, nor unaware of
our sinful behavior. The Lord is intimately aware of
every detail of our lives. King David, in what is considered by many to be the most profound and excellent of
his psalms, says it this way:

> You have searched me, LORD,
>   and you know me.
> You know when I sit and when I rise;
>   you perceive my thoughts from afar.
> You discern my going out and my lying down;
>   you are familiar with all my ways.

Before a word is on my tongue
    you, Lord, know it completely.
You hem me in behind and before,
    and you lay your hand upon me.
Such knowledge is too wonderful for me,
    too lofty for me to attain.

Where can I go from your Spirit?
    Where can I flee from your presence?
If I go up to the heavens, you are there;
    if I make my bed in the depths, you are
        there.
If I rise on the wings of the dawn,
    if I settle on the far side of the sea,
even there your hand will guide me,
    your right hand will hold me fast.
If I say, "Surely the darkness will hide me
    and the light become night around me,"
even the darkness will not be dark to you;
    the night will shine like the day,
    for darkness is as light to you.
    (Ps. 139:1–12)

As Isaiah later discovered, while human beings continuously attempt to hide from God, in the full light of the Lord's glory, nothing is hidden.

"Woe to me . . ."

Undoubtedly, it was an amazing and life-changing experience for Isaiah to see the Lord in all of His glory. But even as he is taking in the majesty and wonder of the moment, Isaiah is simultaneously struck with an awareness of something that is not glorious. In that profound and unimaginable light, he becomes aware of the depths of his own sinfulness. He understands just how much separation there is between his life and

God's righteousness. He sees himself, perhaps for the first time, as he truly is. In the moment that his gaze moves from God's throne to his own inward being, Isaiah is affected deeply and personally. He is shattered and overwrought. In this light, Isaiah realizes there can be no more hiding, no more pious masks, no more religious posturing.

Perhaps Isaiah was remembering this very moment when he later wrote: "All of us have become like one who is unclean, and all our righteous acts are like filthy rags; we all shrivel up like a leaf, and like the wind our sins sweep us away" (Isa. 64:6). It is impossible to know for sure, but we do know that in this moment of self-reflection and self-knowledge, Isaiah was undone. When the realization of who he was in the light of God's perfection became clear to him, he opened his mouth and emitted an earth-shattering Hebrew cry: OY! (pronounced o'-ee).

English translations of Isaiah's Hebrew cry typically translate it: "Woe to me." Unfortunately, this ancient Semitic howl of anguish loses a bit of its force in the translation. The actual exclamation—"oy"—can still be heard in the Middle East today, and is generally the shrieking wail that is heard from someone who has experienced great pain or loss. A mother learning of the death of her child might cry out in anguish using this expression. It is an utterance that stresses the intensity of, and personal engagement with, a particular sorrow.

Isaiah is not casually noting his own blemishes. He is not simply acknowledging the stain of sin in his life and saying softly, "Well, this is embarrassing." He is broken to the core of his being. As he cries out in the pain of his recognition, he also realizes the implications for his life. "I am ruined!" he says. It is as if every sin, every failure, every broken place in his life has been exposed, and he realizes that there is nothing he can do to make himself holy in the light of God's holiness. This moment of enlightened insight was painful and distressing for Isaiah, perhaps the most intense moment of his life to that point. It was also vitally important, for in this moment Isaiah also clearly understood his need.

As awful as this moment is, and as deep as Isaiah's anguish is at the realization of his own sinful state, this too is part of the good news. As is the case with every human being, God needed to bring Isaiah out of his hiding, expose his shame, and bring him into full recognition of his condition in order to begin the process of his redemption. Human beings have always sought to avoid these moments, but the Lord knows how desperately we need them.

Recovering What Was Lost

"In the beginning God created the heavens and the earth" and it was good (see Genesis 1). God spoke and oceans came into being. He said "trees," and the forests of the world were made. He sang songs of life and the animals of the world inhabited the earth. (Someone once said, "God sneezed and we got a duck-billed platypus," but I digress.) All of it was good. Then God took a different approach. Scooping up the soil of the earth, God breathed into it and gave life to a being that He formed in God's own image: a human being. This time God said it was *very* good (Gen. 1:31a, emphasis added)!

God created human beings for relationship, both with Him and with each other. Indeed, the first "not

good" in Scripture concerns the relational needs of
human being: "It is not good for the man to be alone"
(Gen. 2:18). From the outset, God was in close relationship with His human creation. Adam and Eve spent
time in the presence of their Creator without shame
or hiding. God had given them everything they needed
for life and joy. He encouraged them to enjoy the
garden of Eden, and to be fruitful and multiply. He
also instructed them not to eat of the tree of the knowledge of good and evil. That would bring death, God
assured them.

It didn't take long, however, for the serpent to
slither into the garden and try to tempt Adam and Eve
into disobeying God. The challenge for the Enemy
was how to tempt those who already had everything
they needed. God's very good creation had sustenance,
relationship, and the freedom to explore their world
and create new life. What could possibly be missing?
But the serpent was crafty. Instead of offering them
possessions, power, or pleasure, he simply told them
that if they ate the forbidden fruit, their eyes would be
opened, and "you will be like God" (Gen. 3:5).

Imagine the situation: Adam and Eve already had
everything they could possibly want or need. Why
would they even desire to be like God? There really
is only one value they could have perceived in being
like God: in becoming like God themselves, they
would no longer need God! Sin, from the outset, has
always been about rejecting God, pushing God off
the throne, and trying to replace God with our own
forms of godliness. And in the same way Adam and
Eve gave in to temptation, disobeying their Creator in
a vain and futile attempt to be like God, all subsequent
human beings in this fallen world have been subject

to the same temptation. As with our ancestors, we all succumb to the temptation. The results are always the same as well.

From the moment they tasted the forbidden fruit, Adam and Eve knew that they had done something horribly wrong. They realized that something vitally important had changed in their relationship with their Creator. They also understood that they were exposed, and they were ashamed. They responded by attempting to cover their shame and to hide themselves from God. Sin brought separation into the relationship between Creator and creation. And although God came seeking His creatures and showed mercy and care for them when He found them, the image of God in which they were created had been deeply tarnished in ways that were irreparable by human effort alone.

Two serious maladies resulted from this sad episode for all humanity. First, human beings have been trying to be like God ever since. We wear masks of piety, create lesser gods in our own image, and justify our actions with false comparisons. This effort to be our own gods manifests in comments such as, "It's my life and I will live it however I choose to live it. No one is going to tell me what to do."

At some deep level, however, all human beings know that we are not like God, and that we miss the mark. This understanding leads to the second malady, wherein, as with Adam and Eve, we are ashamed and feel exposed, so we hide from God and hope to go unnoticed. When confronted with our own sinfulness, we equivocate, we deny, we blame others, or we compare ourselves to the lowest common denominator. We say things along the lines of, "Hey, I'm a pretty good person. I'm not aware of anything really all that wrong in my life. Besides, I'm better than most people. You wouldn't believe what some of the people I work with are like. Hey, it's not like I'm Hitler." Having set out to deceive God, we end up deceiving ourselves.

Surprisingly, it is the reality of this universal human condition that makes Isaiah's inward look, in the light of God's glory, good news. As we saw in the first chapter, God wants to be found by us. If we seek Him, we will find Him. And when we find Him, God also wants us to know the truth, to look inward, to see ourselves as we really are. This inward knowing, though painful initially, is not meant for our destruction. Instead, it opens us up to freedom, to the restoration of the image of God in us, and to renewing a right relationship with our Creator.

Even the secular philosopher Socrates understood that, "the unexamined life is not worth living." Yet, it seems to be a part of our nature that human beings try to avoid self-reflective and honest introspection at all costs. It is a part of the ongoing fallout of sin in our lives. We convince ourselves that it is somehow better to live in denial, or in obstinate resistance to God's truth about our lives. Yet, the Lord Jesus Himself assures us: "Then you will know the truth, and the truth will set you free" (John 8:32).

Isaiah, even in his agony over how far he was missing the mark, likely found reassurance as he realized that he was not alone in his brokenness. He exclaims, "I live among a people of unclean lips" (Isa. 6:5). He recognizes the same truth that the apostle Paul later shared with the Romans: "for all have sinned and fall short of the glory of God" (Rom. 3:23). This revelation, though deeply disturbing, is also freeing. It reminds us that all human beings are in the same boat, that the serpent was a liar and there really is no one who can be like God, and that we are all in need of divine assistance if we are ever to be able to stand in the glory of God.

In one of the most beautiful ironies of the life of faith, it is in that same painful moment of recognition and honesty, of complete brokenness before God, that we are finally prepared to begin the journey toward restoration. And this moment of recognition, of coming face-to-face with the truth of who we are in the light of God's glory, will come into every life sooner or later. It is only a matter of when and on what terms.

Everything Will See the Light

The late Methodist Bishop Bill Cannon was a great leader and evangelist in the church. He was a dynamic preacher who had memorized the entire New Testament. He was known as a pious and devout believer. He was also a friend for many years with Georgia Governor, and ultimately U.S. President, Jimmy Carter. He is often remembered for giving the opening prayer at President Carter's 1977 inauguration.

I had the memorable experience of hearing Bishop Cannon preach shortly before he died. In that message, he shared the story of an uncomfortable event from his life. In 1976, Jimmy Carter, himself a devout Sunday-school-teaching Baptist, was in the midst of his presidential election. It came as a surprise to nearly everyone that Mr. Carter agreed to do an interview with *Playboy* magazine. Bishop Cannon, very interested in the campaign of his friend, expressed interest in knowing what was said in the interview. He told the story this way:

I was in Atlanta Hartsfield airport when my aide came over and said, "Bishop, that interview is in the new issue of the magazine and it is on the newsstand here." Well, I wanted to read the article but also wanted to be accountable, so I said to my aide, "Here's what you can do. Take my briefcase over to the newsstand. Buy the magazine and slip it into my briefcase. Then when we are on the airplane, you and I can read the interview together. We can also hold each other accountable for not going through the rest of the magazine. Then we'll just dispose of it when we get where we are going, and no one will know anything about it."

Well, wouldn't you know, my aide brought me my briefcase with the magazine inside, and we got in the security line. I went to set my briefcase down on the little belt for it to go through the scanner, and the young lady working the line said, "Oh no sir, I'm sorry, but the machine in broken. We will have to inspect your briefcase by hand." And with that, she opened it right up, and there it was . . . in front of God and everybody![1]

Then Bishop Cannon slipped his reading glasses down, peered over the top of them, looked sternly at all of us, and proclaimed: "My brothers and sisters, be sure your sin will find you out!"

---

1. Bishop William R. Cannon, "Rise Up, O Church: Phil. 3:12–13," Keynote Address, Florida Annual Conference UMC, Lakeland, FL, June 2, 1944.

Of course, he was right. One way or another everything will see the light of day. Jesus said, "There is nothing concealed that will not be disclosed, or hidden that will not be made known. What you have said in the dark will be heard in the daylight, and what you have whispered in the ear in the inner rooms will be proclaimed from the roofs" (Luke 12:2–3). God would like for each of us to come clean with Him on our own, while there is still time to do something about it. It is an act of grace on God's part when He shines the light of His glory into the dark places of our hearts so that we can see what is there . . . and respond.

The Accuser

There is an episode from my life as a teenager of which I am not at all proud. Yet it will be forever burned into my memory. By the time I was sixteen years old, I was living a duplicitous life. I was not walking with the Lord, and I was involved in a number of things that were both illegal and dangerous. I also went to church. I was playing a game with people. I said all the right things to the adults in my life. I put on a good show. The exterior was all bright and looked right, but the interior of my life was dark and disturbing. It was in the midst of this season that I began to sell drugs to my high school friends. I assumed I was smart enough to get away with all of it, and I imagined I had everyone fooled.

As a normal practice I would only sell to people my own age, but I had one friend a couple of years younger than I who wanted to buy some marijuana from me. Our families lived close together. Our parents interacted from time to time. And because I was driving already, his mother would sometimes allow him ride to school and run around with me. She said, "I don't trust him with other people your age, but you are such a fine young man, I trust him with you." Proving that her trust was misplaced, I sold her son the marijuana. A few days later when his mother discovered the drugs, my friend told her everything.

On the evening of the mother's discovery, I was home with my family watching reruns of old sitcoms on TV when our phone rang. As I answered the phone, I heard a cold, angry voice on the other end say, "I know who you are, and I know what you do!" It was, of course, the boy's mother. I quickly replied, "I don't know what you are talking about." Ice cold, she said slowly and clearly, "Don't play innocent with me. I know what you do. And you need to tell your father. You need to come clean with your father. Because if you don't tell him, I will. You have one hour." And she hung up the phone.

I don't know if you are familiar with the expression "when your blood runs cold," but I experienced it fully in that moment. It felt like all the heat, all the life, all the oxygen left my being at once. I stood there in shock; that naked kind of shock that you feel when all of your carefully constructed defenses are gone, and people can see you for who you truly are. I thought about what she had said: "You need to come clean with your father. Because if you don't tell him, I will."

Working up the courage to tell my father is one of the hardest things I have ever had to do. I actually started with my mother because I figured she would be a safety net. That was hard. But it seemed even harder to sit down with my father and look this man in the eyes and tell him I had been living a lie.

My father surprised me though. Oh, there was anger, and there was punishment (I still remember the punishment). But there was also grace . . . because he wanted to kill me, but he didn't. And, despite his anger, he kept on loving me. And he kept on letting me know that I was his son, and that nothing could change that.

I have come back to that moment many times in my mind. As painful and life-changing as it was, and as hard as the consequences were to deal with, it was also an incredibly freeing moment. It freed me from living in the shadows and living a lie. It got the truth out in the open where it could be dealt with. And it actually served to restore some important things in my relationship with my father. My dark night of the soul had become an important part of the good news in my life. I also came to understand that there was a deeper message in the words of my friend's mother: "You need to come clean with your father. Because if you don't tell him, I will."

Humanity has an enemy. He is called many things: Satan, the Enemy, the Devil, evil, and a host of other names. One of the names the Bible uses to describe him is Accuser. By whatever name, he is a power at work in this world who wants to destroy us. He is the same one who lied to Adam and Eve in the garden, who started this entire mess. He knows our secrets, both large and small. He knows who we really are behind all of our religious game playing. And he looks forward to dragging us before our heavenly Father and making his accusations. In a very real sense, the Bible is telling us: "You'd better come clean with your heavenly Father, because if you don't tell Him, the Accuser will."

When we have our "woe to me" moment, when we come clean before our Maker and let Him know that we know the depths of our own depravity and how far short we really fall from the glory of God, we are in that moment thwarting the works of the Enemy in our lives. By coming clean before our Creator, we are negating Satan's power to accuse. And we are, in that instant, in exactly the right place for God to do some of His best work in our lives.

Flee from the Wrath to Come

When Anglican priest John Wesley was establishing his eighteenth-century discipleship movement, a movement that led to a great awakening in the church, he developed one question that was asked of anyone who wanted to be admitted to his societies: "Do you have a desire to flee from the wrath to come?"

Later, the General Rules of the United Societies would put it this way:

> There is only one condition previously required of those who desire admission into these societies, "A desire to flee from the wrath to come, and to be saved from their sins." But wherever this is really fixed in the soul, it will be shown by its fruits. It is therefore expected of all who continue therein that they shall continue to evidence their desire for salvation.[2]

---

2. John Wesley, *The Nature, Design, and General Rules, of the United Societies: In London, Bristol, Kingswood, and Newcastle upon Tyne* (Oxford, UK: Felix Farley, 1747).

Wesley understood that in order to appropriate salvation, it is essential that each of us first understand the true nature of sin within us. Additionally, it is essential to grasp how abhorrent sin is to God, and that the penalty for all sin is death. Wesley understood that while God is loving, and good, and His mercies are new every morning, He is also just. There is a wrath of God directed toward sin. There will be a reckoning.

In John Wesley's sermon entitled "Justification by Faith" he wrote:

> How a sinner may be justified before God, the Lord and Judge of all, is a question of no common importance to every child of man. It contains the foundations of all our hope, inasmuch as while we are at enmity with God, there can be no true peace, no solid joy, either in time or in eternity. What peace can there be, while our own heart condemns us; and much more, He that is "greater than our heart and knoweth all things?" What solid joy, either in this world or that to come, while "the wrath of God abideth on us?"[3]

For those who have their "woe to me" moment and understand the full significance of their standing before God, there is often a heartfelt desire to flee from the wrath to come. This is exactly what John the Baptist was speaking about as he preached, preparing people for the coming of Jesus: "John said to the crowds coming out to be baptized by him, 'You brood

---

3. John Wesley, *The Works of John Wesley*, ed. Albert C. Outler, Sermon 5, "Justification by Faith" (Nashville, TN: Abingdon Press, 1984–2015).

of vipers! Who warned you to flee from the coming
wrath? Produce fruit in keeping with repentance'"
(Luke 3:7–8a).

Isaiah must have felt this desire to flee from the
wrath to come as he cried out, "Woe to me! . . . I am
ruined!" (Isa. 6:5a).

Coming Clean

There are several markers in the life of one who desires
to flee from the wrath to come. The first is confession. Isaiah's immediate response when he looked
inward and saw himself in the light of God's glory was
to confess that he was unclean. His confession was
personal. He does note that he is part of an unclean
people, but only after his personal confession. Even
as he confesses, Isaiah must realize that God already
knows everything about him. Nothing Isaiah declares
is going to come as a surprise to the Lord. His confession of his own uncleanness, however, lets God know
that he sees it, and is willing to be honest before God
about who he is.

It is widely understood that confession is good
for the soul. It is a regular, ongoing process for those
who walk in the light. The need for confession is not
limited to those who are coming clean with God for
the first time. The apostle John said to the faithful
believers in the church: "If we claim to be without sin,
we deceive ourselves and the truth is not in us. If we
confess our sins, he is faithful and just and will forgive
us our sins and purify us from all unrighteousness"
(1 John 1:8–9). Even those who are devoted followers
of Jesus need regular, ongoing times of confession in
their lives.

In the early Wesleyan movement, made up of those who had a desire to flee the coming wrath, band meetings quickly became an important feature. These groups consisted of approximately five people who met regularly to mutually confess their sins and struggles, and encourage each other in their walks of faith. Band meetings were a central part of the movement, and confession was a core component of these gatherings. Members talked specifically about their temptations, successes, and failures. Creating an intentional and mutually accountable space for confession was considered essential to the process of growing in personal holiness. Wesleyan believers understood the need for ongoing confession in their lives.

A second marker in the life of one who desires to flee from the wrath to come is repentance. John the Baptist exhorted those coming to him in the wilderness to "produce fruit in keeping with repentance" (Matt. 3:8). In order to be effective, confession and repentance must go hand in hand. God is not surprised by the sin we confess. As David pointed out in Psalm 139, God already has a clear understanding of all that is going on in our lives. In confession, we let God know that we recognize and acknowledge what He already knows about us. Admitting our shortcomings is one thing; however, being troubled by them is something else entirely.

I recall an old revival preacher saying many years ago, "Repentance is not being sorry. Repentance is being sorry enough to quit!" Biblical repentance, though, is much deeper than being sorry, even being sorry enough to quit. The word *repentance* literally means "to turn around," to reorient our focus. It is no surprise that repentance follows our looking up and seeing the Lord. Having discovered the presence of the glory of God, repentance is a reorientation from a life moving away from God (or hiding from God) to a life moving toward God. To live a repentant life requires fixing our eyes upon Jesus, and constantly returning our gaze to Him when we discover that it has drifted to lesser things. It is an ongoing process.

John Wesley was aware that some people, having been touched by conviction, confess their sins and their desire to flee from the wrath to come, but do not actually move into true repentance. In his sermon "The Spirit of Bondage and Adoption," he noted of these people, "They feel the burden of sin, and earnestly desire to flee from the wrath to come. But not long: They seldom suffer the arrows of conviction to go deep into their souls; but quickly stifle the grace of God, and return to their wallowing in the mire."[4]

Repentance is less of a response of guilt, and more of a desire to move toward the beauty, purity, and holiness of God. When Isaiah notices his own predicament in light of God's glory, he is, of course, ashamed. He is simultaneously in reverential awe of the Lord. He is drawn to the glory of the Lord, and desires to orient his life in that direction. Fleeing from the wrath to come can be an initial catalyst, nudging a person away from sin. But it is the desire to flee toward the glory, holiness, majesty, wonder, and grace of God that keeps us going . . . if we fix our eyes on Him.

---

4. John Wesley, *The Works of John Wesley*, ed. Albert C. Outler, sermon 9, "The Spirit of Bondage and Adoption" (Nashville, TN: Abingdon Press, 1984–2015).

The final marker of one who desires to flee from the wrath to come is living a life of sincerity. The apostle Paul tells the church in Corinth: "Now this is our boast: Our conscience testifies that we have conducted ourselves in the world, and especially in our relations with you, with integrity and godly sincerity. We have done so, relying not on worldly wisdom but on God's grace" (2 Cor. 1:12). Godly sincerity, in this context, means purity. The term has an interesting history that sheds some light on why it is important. The Greek word Paul uses is *eilikrines*, which is translated as "sincerity." The word is essentially a combination of two other Greek words: *heile*, meaning "sunlight" and *krino*, meaning "judge" or even "condemn." Thus, the word implies something that, though perhaps looking good in the shadows, is best brought into the full light of the day to be judged; either valued for its purity or condemned as a forgery or fraud. Therefore, in the sense in which Paul is speaking, living a life of godly sincerity means keeping our lives in the full light of God's glory where it can be judged for its purity. Paul assures the Corinthian church that he has tried to live this way among them. This is exactly where Isaiah found himself as well.

The English word *sincere* is also interesting. Although the origin of the word is debated, there is much oral history that suggests it is the combination of two Latin words: *sine*, meaning "without" and *cera*, meaning "wax." The word is said to have come into usage in the 1500s when sculptors sometimes created cheap knockoffs of major works of art. As the cheaper versions had many imperfections, the sculptors would

sometimes mix marble dust with wax and fill in the
flaws. In the weak indoor light and in the shadows,
it was often hard to discover the flaws. But when the
sculptures were brought into the direct sunlight, the
wax would begin to melt and the flaws were exposed.
Thus, to be sincere, or "without wax" meant to be
authentic, pure, and without hidden flaws that would
be exposed in the light.

It is exactly this sense in which we are called to
live in the light. To live a life of sincerity means living
in the light, with a desire to be pure and authentic, not
covering or hiding away our flaws, but exposing them
to the light in openness to God.

Not a One-and-Done Process

This process of exposing our hearts to the light of God's
glory—confessing what we see there, repenting, and
moving into godly sincerity—is not a one-time deal. As
we saw earlier from the apostle John, confession is a
regular part of a believer's life. John also assured us:
"But if we walk in the light, as he is in the light, we have
fellowship with one another, and the blood of Jesus, his
Son, purifies us from all sin" (1 John 1:7). But walking
in the light means that more and more of our lives will
be exposed to the light, so that we may be purified. King
David said, "You have set our iniquities before you, our
secret sins in the light of your presence" (Ps. 90:8). In
the light of God, our secret sins are exposed more and
more the closer we move to the Lord.

Consider the sanctified life of the apostle Paul.
He was certainly moving from glory to glory into the
very image of Jesus. Indeed, he eventually became so

close to the Lord that he could say with confidence, "Follow my example, as I follow the example of Christ" (1 Cor. 11:1). Yet, notice the progression of his self-assessment in the light of God's ever-present glory with him: To the church at Corinth, he is the "least of the apostles." ("For I am the least of the apostles and do not even deserve to be called an apostle, because I persecuted the church of God" [1 Cor. 15:9].)

By the time of the letter to the church at Ephesus, he is the "least of all the Lord's people." ("Although I am less than the least of all the Lord's people, this grace was given me: to preach to the Gentiles the boundless riches of Christ" [Eph. 3:8].)

Finally, in his letter to Timothy, he has become "the worst of sinners." ("But for that very reason I was shown mercy so that in me, the worst of sinners, Christ Jesus might display his immense patience as an example for those who would believe in him and receive eternal life" [1 Tim. 1:16].)

We should not assume from this example that Paul was somehow becoming less holy or less righteous as he walked with the Lord. Quite the contrary, the closer he grew to the Lord, the more clearly he saw himself. With that clear understanding of who he was, Paul also understood just how far he was from the holiness of God. He also knew that he was moving in the direction of the Lord, and that the Holy Spirit was moving him from glory to glory. That understanding was the source of great hope and joy for Paul, and made his "woe to me" moments an important element of the gospel, the good news, in his life.

Our Own "Woe to Me" Moment

It is vital that we understand that no one can hide from God forever. Into every life the "woe to me" moment will come. The only question is: Will that moment come when we seek the face of God and invite His light into our lives, or when the Enemy, the Accuser, drags us before the throne of God and claims, "This one belongs to me"? The good news is, we get to choose.

When we are confronted with our "woe to me" moments, despite the anguish we feel in being exposed, it can be a wonderful good-news moment if it prompts us to confession, repentance, and a desire to live lives of sincerity. And if we begin with a desire to flee from the wrath to come, the good news is that the Lord is always there, beckoning us with His grace. Because of that grace, we can flee from death straight into the life-giving light of our Lord.

FOUR

You Are the Man!

Search me, God, and know my heart; test me and know my anxious thoughts. See if there is any offensive way in me, and lead me in the way everlasting.

—PSALM 139:23–24

Can you imagine hearing God refer to you as "a man (or woman) after my own heart"? To be judged by our Creator in that way would be amazingly affirming, signifying a life well lived. And that is exactly what God said about young David, the shepherd boy in whom God saw a king: "After removing Saul, he made David their king. God testified concerning him: 'I have found David son of Jesse, a man after my own heart; he will do everything I want him to do'" (Acts 13:22).

There was certainly much to be admired in David. He was an extraordinary man. Remarkably, he is still revered today, several thousand years after his death, not only by Jewish faithful, but by Muslims and Christians as well. His tomb is one of the most sacred sites in modern-day Israel, visited by thousands of pilgrims each year.

Born into a shepherding family in Bethlehem, David was the youngest boy of eight sons and two daughters. As the runt of the family, he was so insignificant that his father Jesse didn't even think to call him in when the prophet Samuel showed up to anoint one of his sons as king. Yet even as a youth he began to stand out. David's gifts were both eclectic and remarkable. Early on he was a talented musician whose songs were so beautiful they were able to soothe King Saul's raging heart. While he was still too small to wear an adult's armor, he proved to be a valiant warrior as he bravely slew the Philistine giant Goliath in individual combat.

He matured into a renowned leader with whom the greatest people of his day desired to serve. Upon becoming king, he led his people in battle, subdued all of Israel's enemies, and unified the people of Israel. Yet he found time for writing poetry so beautiful and compelling that it is still beloved around the world today.

David was such a statesman that he is generally credited with founding the nation of Israel, and even today his star adorns the nation's flag. And the Bible reports that he was so beautiful and charismatic that pretty much everyone was attracted to him. He is so important biblically that sixty-six chapters of the Bible are devoted to his story. Abraham, by comparison, has fourteen chapters. The great prophet Elijah, only ten. By the world's standards, David was quite a man.

Despite this stellar résumé, however, David was also a deeply flawed human being. He willfully, and with much devious planning, committed adultery with the wife of one of his most loyal servants. Then in a clumsy attempt to cover over his sin, he arranged for that same faithful man to be killed in battle. He was often capricious, as well as self-indulgent. He ran with outlaws and thieves. He had so much blood on his hands that God would not allow him to build a temple in His honor. He was an indulgent parent who often failed to correct his children and was forced to deal with outright rebellion by various sons on multiple occasions. And he sometimes ignored godly counsel from his advisers with disastrous consequences. In short, this is not exactly the portrait most of us create in our minds of a man after God's own heart. Yet that is exactly who God said that David was.

In the book of Acts, Luke tells us: "Now when David had served God's purpose in his own generation, he fell asleep; he was buried with his ancestors and his body decayed" (Acts 13:36). So how did this complicated, imperfect man come to be known as a man after God's own heart and as one who served God's purpose for his generation?

Despite his power and the multitude of responsibilities he had and the challenges he faced, David made a habit of three important practices that kept his heart centered in God.

- First, he opened his heart regularly to the light of God's glory. In a similar fashion to Isaiah, he looked inward and saw himself as God saw him and as he truly was.
- Second, he regularly acknowledged and confessed his personal sins and failures, and was appropriately humble and repentant before God.

- Finally, he developed an accountable relationship with a godly counselor and opened himself to correction on a regular basis.

Practice Makes Perfect

These three practices assured that his sins and failures did not derail his walk with God, nor define his life. In this way, he was unlike the king who preceded him and many who came after him as well.

Let's look closely at how these practices played out in David's life.

Search Me!

Psalm 139 opens with the assertion that God has searched us and knows us. It goes into great detail concerning the depths of God's knowledge of us, and our utter inability to hide from God's presence. The psalm then concludes with an invitation: "Search me, God, and know my heart; test me and know my anxious thoughts. See if there is any offensive way in me, and lead me in the way everlasting" (vv. 23–24).

God already knows everything there is to know about David. The great king knows that as well. He is aware that God knit him together in his mother's womb, and has been intimately aware of his thoughts and actions for all of his life. David has a deep desire for God to shine the light of His glory into the deepest, darkest places of his own heart. He wants God to inspect his inner life and to make David aware of anything offensive that lies within him. Like Isaiah,

David is willing to face up to who he truly is, in the light of God.

In 2001, I was having lunch with Pastor Wayne Cordeiro, the founding pastor of New Hope Christian Fellowship in Hawaii, discussing the possibility of me becoming the teaching pastor at New Hope. I asked Pastor Wayne if he had any questions for me as we considered this possible ministry calling. He paused briefly and then replied, "There is only one thing that I'm interested in right now. How is your inner conversation?" I admit the question caught me off guard. I asked Pastor Wayne if he could elaborate a bit. He then said:

> Max, it is an easy thing to dress up the outside. You can buy a pair of nice slacks, carry a Bible, work up a good sermon or two, and be kind to people. You can look the part of a godly man and a sound pastor. But I'm not all that interested in the outside. That's easy to do. I want to know what is going on inside you when you are alone with God and your own inner thoughts. What is the inner conversation you have in the dark? How are things with you and the Lord when you are not "on" and it is just the two of you?

Both Pastor Wayne and King David were getting at an important truth. David's son Solomon would later make that truth explicit: "For as he thinks in his heart, so is he" (Prov. 23:7 NKJV). It is good for people to not only look inward on a regular basis, but to invite the Lord to look inward with us, to search our hearts and know us. And then to spend those quiet times alone with the Lord, asking for Him to show us what He knows of us.

David was undoubtedly an introspective person. His music and poetry reveal a thoughtful heart. It is therefore likely that David already knew much of what the Lord would find and show him. But the great king understood another human reality, one that Jeremiah subsequently learned: "The heart is deceitful above all things and beyond cure. Who can understand it?" (Jer. 17:9). Human beings regularly lie to themselves. We live in denial. We equivocate. We make excuses. We attribute false motives to our actions. We hide our true selves, not only from God, but often from others and even ourselves. It is part of the universal condition. David is inviting God to show him that to which he is blind, whether willfully or unintentionally so.

A person after God's own heart will always have a heart's desire to be righteous, and to be in a clean, pure relationship with God. But because of the inherent deceptiveness in our human nature, our desire will never be enough. We need the help of our Maker, who knows us as only the one who created us can know us. Everyone benefits from periodic self-assessments, but regular God-assessments are even more valuable.

Daily Meditation

So how does God search us? Through what means does the Lord show us when there is any offensive way within us? At times God uses other godly women and men to speak with those who are seeking Him. We will discuss that idea later in this chapter. God typically speaks most directly to us, however, through prayer and meditation on His Word.

David was a man of deep and persistent prayer. He prayed in a variety of ways. He sought the Lord's counsel. He cried out to the Lord for help. He meditated on the wonders of the Lord. He interceded on behalf of others. He prayed prayers of confession and lamentation. And he meditated on the Word of God.

The apostle Paul notes several categories of prayer in his first letter to Timothy: "I urge, then, first of all, that petitions, prayers, intercession and thanksgiving be made for all people—" (1 Tim. 2:1).

Note that Paul speaks of prayer in four different ways:

- Petitions, also called "supplications" in some English translations, are those fervent requests we make to God around specific needs in our lives. David often prayed prayers of supplication. God's answers to those prayers are usually self-evident.
- Intercession involves crying out to the Lord on behalf of others. Again, David made a habit of intercession, especially on behalf of the people of Israel.
- Thanksgiving is fairly self-explanatory. The psalms of David are filled with expressions of Thanksgiving and praise for who God is and what God has done, indicating a life that was over-flowing with sincere thanksgiving and praise. All three of these forms of communication with God are important. They are not, however, the primary means God uses to search us and know us.
- In his list, in addition to petitions, intercessions, and thanksgiving, Paul also lists prayers. When the apostle uses prayers in this sense, he obviously means something other than petitions,

intercessions, and thanksgiving. Yet, for many believers, our prayers consist largely, sometimes even exclusively, of these three things.

What, then, is this prayer that Paul encourages that is substantially different from the other three? I would contend that it involves meditation on God, on the things of God, and particularly on God's Word. This kind of prayerful meditation was not only a regular practice in David's life, it was also a primary means through which God could search David's heart and communicate with him.

Prayer is generally understood to be our communication with God. In practice, however, it is far too often a one-sided monologue. With petition, intercession, and thanksgiving, we are usually talking to God. Monologues hardly constitute communication in the best sense of the word. One-sided communication is not only less than effective, at the end of the day it can barely be said to be communication at all. Meditation on the things of God and on God's Word, however, is decidedly different. In it, we make space for God to speak to us. When we do so, God does speak. The Psalms give evidence that David practiced prayerful meditation with great regularity and just as regularly heard the Lord speaking to him.

Consider the following passages from David's psalms:

When I consider your heavens,
     the work of your fingers,
the moon and the stars,
     which you have set in place,
what is mankind that you are mindful of
          them,

human beings that you care for them?
    (Ps. 8:3–4)

On my bed I remember you;
    I think of you through the watches of
        the night.
Because you are my help,
    I sing in the shadow of your wings.
        (Ps. 63:6–7)

The heavens declare the glory of God;
the skies proclaim the work of his hands.
    (Ps. 19:1)

In each of these passages, and in many others, David shows us how he has considered the works of God, creation itself, and the character of God. He has meditated on these things and, in doing so, heard the voice of God.

The one particular practice, however, that rises above them all is meditation on the Word of God.

Blessed is the one
    who does not walk in step with
        the wicked
or stand in the way that sinners take
    or sit in the company of mockers,
but whose delight is in the law of the Lord,
    and who meditates on his law day
        and night.
That person is like a tree planted by streams
        of water,
    which yields its fruit in season
and whose leaf does not wither—
    whatever they do prospers. (Ps. 1:1–3)

> I rise before dawn and cry for help;
>> I have put my hope in your word.
> My eyes stay open through the watches of
>> the night,
>> that I may meditate on your promises.
>> (Ps. 119:147–48)

Notice that David describes meditating on the law of God "day and night." He speaks of rising "before dawn," crying for help and putting his trust in God's Word. He tells of lying awake in the deep of the night meditating on the promises of God. It is in these moments, when prayer is about so much more than speaking words to God, and includes listening for the still, small voice of God, that David allows his heart to be searched by the Lord.

In 2008, the interdenominational megachurch Willow Creek spent three million dollars developing a survey (called Reveal) to measure, among other things, which spiritual practices contribute most to spiritual growth in Christian disciples. The ultimate Reveal report had enough data to fill several books. There were lots of insights. But there was one particular finding that stood out above all the rest. Of all the spiritual practices measured, daily meditation on the Word of God was by far the most influential catalyst of spiritual growth in the life of a believer. Nothing else came even close. Further, this practice remained influential and important regardless of how long a person had been a disciple or at what stage of discipleship the people were. It is important to note that both reading the Bible and Bible study were also on the list. But those two practices and other similar ones had nowhere near the impact that is associated with daily meditation on the Word of God.

Daily meditation on the Word of God is about coming to the Bible expecting the Lord to speak. It is approaching the text the same way the prophet Eli told young Samuel to approach the Lord: "Speak, LORD, for your servant is listening" (1 Sam. 3:9). It is about holding Scripture up as a mirror to your heart and asking the Lord, "How do You want my heart and my life to be different today as a result of what You speak to me here?" It requires reading slowly and attentively through a particular text, thinking about what is there, and staying with it until the Lord speaks a personal word. And, of course, it is about listening.

There are many reasons people come to the Word of God. Some come for information. And there is obviously much information to be found there. The Bible is filled with useful information and can be a source of great wisdom, but that is not the primary purpose of God's Word.

Others come for inspiration, something that is often found in Scripture. How moving it can be to remember the words of Psalm 23 or the Lord's Prayer! But that, too, is not the main reason for Scripture.

There is a much higher purpose for the Bible than information or inspiration. Scripture is given to God's people primarily for their transformation. When a faithful woman or man meditates on the Word of God with a heart open to hearing a personal word from the Lord, it is often a transformational experience.

This form of Scripture meditation has little in common with Eastern religion meditation practices with their chanting, mantras, and mindlessness. To meditate on Scripture, our souls need time and space to reflect upon what our minds have taken in. Our hearts rejoice as we begin to hear and understand what God is speaking to us, personally. We really meditate when we read carefully, prayerfully consider what is there, and then humbly rely upon what God has revealed to us with a conscious eye toward obedience. All of this, of course, is carried out in complete dependence on the Holy Spirit.

King David was a man after God's own heart, in part, because he practiced daily meditation on God's works and God's Word. In doing so, he not only enabled the Lord to search his heart and see if there was anything offensive in him (see Psalm 139:23–24), he also allowed the Lord to continually cleanse and form his heart.

You Are the Man!

Of course, even with his daily meditations on the things of God, David had sin in his life, some of it particularly vile. The most egregious episode was likely his adulterous relationship with Bathsheba. It is noteworthy that this whole series of events began when David became lax in his personal discipline and sense of duty. The story begins this way: "In the spring, at the time when kings go off to war, David sent Joab out with the king's men and the whole Israelite army. They destroyed the Ammonites and besieged Rabbah. But David remained in Jerusalem" (2 Sam. 11:1). Until this moment, David, the warrior king, had led his armies in battle. But for reasons that are not explained, this particular spring "at the time when kings go off to war," David stayed home while others went off to fight his battles for him. One can only wonder whether his spiritual disciplines had become lax during this season as well. The events that follow make it seem likely that they had.

While the armies were away, the king, lounging in his palace, spied a beautiful young woman bathing on her own rooftop. With lust in his heart, and full knowledge that she was the wife of one of his most loyal and trusted soldiers, David sent for the beautiful Bathsheba and had his way with her. Later, when Bathsheba let him know that she was bearing the king's child, David began a series of devious schemes designed to cover up his sin. One scheme led to another until David finally orchestrated the death of Uriah, Bathsheba's husband, in a hastily contrived battle designed specifically to kill him. And despite King David's closeness to God and growing knowledge of the ways of God, he naively believed that he had fooled everyone and gotten away with his sinful behavior. According to Scripture, however, and as David should have known, the thing that he did displeased the Lord.

In this instance the Lord used another godly man, the prophet Nathan, to show David the error of his ways:

> The LORD sent Nathan to David. When he came to him, he said, "There were two men in a certain town, one rich and the other poor. The rich man had a very large number of sheep and cattle, but the poor man had nothing except one little ewe lamb he had bought. He raised it, and it grew up with him and his children. It shared his food, drank from his cup and even slept in his arms. It was like a daughter to him.

"Now a traveler came to the rich man,
but the rich man refrained from taking one
of his own sheep or cattle to prepare a meal
for the traveler who had come to him. Instead,
he took the ewe lamb that belonged to the
poor man and prepared it for the one who had
come to him."

David burned with anger against the man
and said to Nathan, "As surely as the LORD
lives, the man who did this must die! He must
pay for that lamb four times over, because he
did such a thing and had no pity."

Then Nathan said to David, "You are the
man!" (2 Sam. 12:1–7a)

I have often marveled at the courage of Nathan.
It could not have been easy to look into the eyes of his
king, an immensely powerful man, and tell him, "You
are the man!" It is one of the all-time great confron-
tational accountability stories. Having uttered those
words, Nathan must have wondered what kind of
response he would get.

In nearly every case, David's predecessor on the
throne of Israel, King Saul, when confronted with
his own sinful behavior, had equivocated, lied, made
excuses, or simply refused to listen to the truth. Often,
he had punished the truth tellers. This same sort of
behavior was common among the line of kings who
would follow David when confronted with their own
sin. But this moment with Nathan, a defining moment
in David's life, is what separated him from lesser men.
"Then David said to Nathan, 'I have sinned against the
LORD'" (2 Sam. 12:13).

David could have denied. He could have tried more
ways to cover over his sin. He could even have ordered
Nathan killed. Instead, he immediately confesses his
guilt, and goes into deep mourning, not because he
has been exposed, but because he has failed the Lord.
In David's confession and repentance, he also pens
one of the most open and honest prayers of confession
ever written:

Have mercy on me, O God,
    according to your unfailing love;
according to your great compassion
    blot out my transgressions.
Wash away all my iniquity
    and cleanse me from my sin.

For I know my transgressions,
    and my sin is always before me.
Against you, you only, have I sinned
    and done what is evil in your sight;
so you are right in your verdict
    and justified when you judge.
Surely I was sinful at birth,
    sinful from the time my mother
        conceived me.
Yet you desired faithfulness even in
        the womb;
    you taught me wisdom in that
        secret place.

Cleanse me with hyssop, and I will be clean;
    wash me, and I will be whiter than snow.
Let me hear joy and gladness;
    let the bones you have crushed rejoice.
Hide your face from my sins

and blot out all my iniquity.

Create in me a pure heart, O God,
    and renew a steadfast spirit within me.
Do not cast me from your presence
    or take your Holy Spirit from me.
Restore to me the joy of your salvation
    and grant me a willing spirit, to sustain
        me. (Ps. 51:1–12)

In a similar manner to that of Isaiah, when David willingly brings himself into the presence of God, he is also undone. Notice the nature of his confession and prayer. He acknowledges that he knows what he has done. He admits to the Lord that it was against Him that he had sinned. He sets this sin in the context of an utterly sinful life. He lets the Lord know that he sees exactly who he is, and the depths of his own depravity. But he also acknowledges who God is. He calls on God's unfailing love and compassion. He seeks cleansing from God, knowing that God can do in him what he is unable to do for himself. And then, in his magnificent prayer, he invites God into his heart to do God's redemptive, restorative work. David is not simply seeking a get-out-of-jail-free card. He is not just asking the Lord to forgive and forget his transgression. He is inviting the Lord to work in him, to cleanse his heart, to send forth God's Spirit, and to give David a cooperative and willing spirit in order that he might be transformed. David does not simply want to get off the hook for what he has done. He wants to be back in right relationship with his Lord. Nothing less will do. And David is willing to do whatever the Lord needs him to do, and to submit to whatever the Lord wants to do in his heart, in order to experience that transformation. That is a picture of a man after God's own heart.

Hold Me Accountable

Even those of us who invite the Lord to search our hearts, and who regularly confess our sins and failures and repent before God, can still miss God. That is why David's practice of inviting godly people to speak counsel into his life and to hold him accountable is of such importance. There were many people in the king's life with whom he had this kind of relationship. As a young man, King Saul's son Jonathan played that role. David had his thirty "mighty warriors" (see 2 Samuel 23:8–38), and his wives, and even Hushai the Archite, whom the Bible refers to as "the king's friend" (1 Chron. 27:33 HCSB). But no one played a more important role in this regard than the prophet Nathan.

Nathan plays a number of important roles in David's kingdom. He is instrumental in confirming David's kingship. As we saw with the Bathsheba story, he was willing to rebuke David's abuse of power. And toward the end of David's life, he took the lead in arranging for Solomon's succession. All of these episodes show why Nathan was a great accountability partner for King David.

The idea of allowing someone else to hold us accountable for our lives and actions is threatening to many people. It is vitally important, therefore, that we have a healthy relationship with anyone who will serve us in this way. Nathan not only remained faithful and present in David's life, he also maintained an honest and close relationship. According to the

Chronicler, Nathan ultimately wrote David's life story (see 1 Chronicles 29:29). He had paid close attention to the details of David's life and demonstrated a great love for David.

It is equally important, however, for an accountability counselor in our lives to love the Lord and have a solid relationship with God. Nathan clearly puts God, and God's Word, in first place in his life. When the Word of God and the plans of God contradict the king and his plans, Nathan sides with the Lord.

When David has eliminated his rivals, defeated the Philistines, and established Jerusalem as Israel's capital, he brings the ark of the covenant to Jerusalem. The king then begins to dream of building a temple to honor God and to house the ark. When David shares this plan with Nathan, the prophet initially supports the idea. Shortly thereafter, however, Nathan hears a different word from the Lord. He returns to the king to deliver that word: David will not be allowed to build a temple. According to God, David has too much blood on his hands. Instead, God will make David great, give him success in battle, and establish his royal line. David's son will inherit his throne and build God's temple.

What is most remarkable about the relationship between David and Nathan is David's willingness to receive the counsel and even the rebuke of Nathan, and to act on what Nathan shares with him. Accountability works best when it is invited and encouraged by the recipient, and when it flows from healthy relationship. All of these prerequisites were present between David and Nathan. By allowing himself to be accountable to Nathan, David is able to see some of the most

potentially devastating moments in his life redeemed
by the Lord. He is able to avoid falling deeper and irre-
trievably into sin. Some of his worst impulses are cut
short before he can even act on them. And, because of
the depth of the relationship, Nathan comes to know
David's heart so well that even as the king lies dying,
Nathan is able to help bring about God's purposes in
David's life.

As David lies close to death, Nathan works to
secure the throne for Solomon, David and Bathsheba's
second son. Nathan understood and agreed with David
that Solomon was God's apparent choice to succeed
David. The king's older son Adonijah had attempted
to find his own supporters and make himself king.
Nathan develops a plan, opposes Adonijah, and, with
the help of Bathsheba and others, delivers the throne
to Solomon.

One can scarcely imagine the course of David's
life without the wise counsel and courageous interven-
tion of the prophet Nathan. Yet, all of that was made
possible largely because of David's understanding of
the need to be accountable to others, and his willingness to both invite Nathan to hold him accountable
and to accept his counsel.

Everyone Needs a Nathan

There is not a person alive who is able to hear clearly
and obey completely the voice of the Lord in their own
lives. We misunderstand. We confuse other voices, or
our own personal whims, for the voice of the Lord.
Sometimes when we hear clearly and know with
certainty what God is saying to us, we may still find

obedience challenging, if not impossible. We explain away our lack of obedience, or attempt to find some justification for doing exactly what we wanted to do all along. When we choose other godly women and men and invite them to enter our lives and hold us accountable to the things of God, we benefit from God's ability to use and speak through others as He searches our hearts.

There are some key things to consider when looking for your own Nathan. It is essential to find someone who genuinely loves you, but who loves the Lord even more. We need someone who loves the truth and knows the truth, a person deeply rooted in the Word of God. And, finally, someone who is willing to hold us accountable and willing to speak the hard truth, in love, when it needs to be spoken. As Paul said to the church at Ephesus: "Instead, speaking the truth in love, we will in all things grow up into him who is the Head, that is, Christ" (Eph. 4:15 NIV 1984).

Once one or more people are identified as potential accountability partners, it is important to make the nature of the relationship explicit. Be open and honest about what is sought and what kind of relationship is desired. Put the words together and write a covenant. Specifically give permission to them to speak truth into your life. And be sure to carefully select those to whom you will be accountable. Be wary of those who would self-select and volunteer to hold you accountable. Most true Nathans are reluctant to barge in where they are not invited.

Finally, it is critical to be open and willing to accept the counsel of your accountability partners. It is fascinating to note how Solomon followed his father's pattern in this practice. Nathan had two sons, Azariah and Zabud. Solomon was renowned for being the wisest man to ever live, and perhaps one of the reasons for that was what he had learned from his father. In the scriptural accounting of Solomon's court, we read the following: "Azariah son of Nathan—in charge of the district governors; Zabud son of Nathan—a priest and adviser to the king" (1 Kings 4:5). Solomon continued the tradition of seeking counsel and accountability. He would later write: "The way of fools seems right to them, but the wise listen to advice" (Prov. 12:15).

Thirty Years of Accountability

In the summer of 1990, a group of young pastors in Florida who were in the earliest years of their respective ministries began discussing the formation of a covenant group. The idea was to gather a small group of pastors who loved the Lord, who loved the church, and who loved people. Each had a heart for serving the Lord well in ministry, and a desire to do so while maintaining personal integrity, a strong healthy family life, and a commitment to finishing well. I was honored to be invited to be a part of this group. Right from the beginning the group hammered out a covenant that included regularly gathering for face-to-face meetings, intentionally doing life and ministry together, and holding one another accountable in love.

We understood that accountability had to flow out of genuine love and relationship, and that would be built over time and with intentionality. From the earliest days, we have committed to meeting together for seventy-two hours in retreat twice a year. We agreed to prioritize these times, and with the exception of unforeseeable emergencies, to be present with each other. Through the years, as cell phones and other distractions have become ubiquitous, we have had to revisit what it means to be present with each other, but we have always kept the value of our mutual relationships as a priority. When we gather, we pray together and play together. We eat together (to be honest, we eat *a lot* together) and we worship together. We build memories and we also, individually, share with the rest of the group how it is with our souls. Between our retreat gatherings we also attend conferences together, engage with each other's families and significant life events, and since the advent of cell phones with text streams, have maintained a text group that permits daily communication with each other. We have attended the weddings and funerals of each other's family members, celebrated significant milestones in each other's lives, and wept and mourned together in some of the lowest points in each of our journeys. In short, we do life together, in all its beautiful and ugly complexity.

We also take the accountability seriously. Over the last thirty years each of the seven members of the group have had multiple experiences of being on the receiving end of "hearing the truth in love." We have had our covenant brothers up in our faces, challenging us to look more deeply at some aspect of our lives or ministries. And we have all had our "You are the man!" moments. But because these moments have occurred in an environment of love, healthy relationship, and mutually agreed upon accountability, they have been life-giving rather than destructive. And I have no doubt that each of us has been pulled back from the precipice on numerous occasions.

All of the members of our group began their years of ordained ministry in the mid-1980s. Through the ensuing decades we have watched as, one after another, multitudes of our colleagues in ministry have burned out, quit in discouragement, fallen due to some moral or ethical failing, lost their spouses in crumbling marriages, or simply drifted away from their first love. In every case these events are heart-breaking. One common denominator in far too many of these situations is a lack of accountable relation-ship in many of their lives. The members of our group, however, all still serve prevailing churches or minis-tries that are healthy and making disciples; we are all in healthy decades-long marriages; all still deeply in love with the Lord and called to ministry in His name; and all committed to trying to finish well. And I know, because I have heard each one say so, each of us believes that apart from the relationship, account-ability, and counsel from our covenant brothers, all of us would have fallen by the wayside long ago.

I am grateful for the role these men play in my life. I can't imagine doing life and ministry without them. I am also grateful for the many ways God is able to use them and their counsel to answer my own "Search me, God" prayers. God often speaks through the counsel of these godly men.

Don't Avoid the Inward Look

Unpleasant though they may be, our dark nights of the soul are essential to the abundant life the Lord wants to give us. For many people today, discussion of sin, of "fleeing from the wrath to come," of confes-sion and accountability to God and to others, all seem like archaic and unnecessary discussions. We love the thought of Jesus as our friend (and He is!). We relish the idea that God is love (and He is!). We are uplifted by the idea that the Holy Spirit is our comforter (and He is!). But no good parent attempts to rear a child without discipline. And helping our children come to a true understanding of who they really are is one of the most important gifts we can give them.

Those who desire to skip the soul searching, the confession, the repentance, and the heart searching and go straight to salvation often discover that they have no idea why they would need a savior in the first place. It is part of God's unfailing love and mercy that He enables us to see ourselves as we truly are, and to understand how helpless we are in the face of the overwhelming distance between us and God's holiness. Because in doing so, God creates in us a need for a power greater than any we possess to save us. And that is a need God is willing and able to fulfill.

In chapter 2 we remembered the words Robert Burns wrote: "O wad some Power the giftie gie us, to see oursels as ithers see us!" As powerful as Burns's sentiment is, I would go further: "Oh would some Power the gift give us, to see ourselves as God sees us." Thankfully, for those who will invite God to join them in the inward look, that is a gift God willingly grants.

FIVE

The Outward Look

With [the coal] he touched my mouth and said, "See, this has touched your lips; your guilt is taken away and your sin atoned for."

—ISAIAH 6:7

Y ou should surf Makaha with me someday soon. You would like that!"

I was talking with Pastor Roy Yamamoto, one of my colleagues at New Hope in Hawaii, and the head of the church's prison ministry and outreach. At six-foot-two, with a chiseled 240-pound frame, this soft-spoken leader was a gentle giant. I had just shared with him about a weekend surf trip to another part of the island when he mentioned Makaha. I was certain he was right; I would love to surf there. The surf break at Makaha is world famous and produces a much sought-after wave.

There was just one problem. Roy was a local, well-known on the island and in the very localized communities on the leeward side where Makaha is located. I was the exact opposite; a middle-aged pasty-white pastor from the mainland with marginal surfing skills at best. Makaha is known as a "locals only" surf break. Though it is possible for outsiders to surf there, the beach has a well-established pecking order among the locals. Outsiders are at the bottom of the stack, and even then, need to earn their place. Someone like me is typically encouraged to respect the locals and seek waves elsewhere. I chuckled a bit nervously and said, "Roy, do you really think it is a good idea for me to paddle out at Makaha? I mean, seriously, look at me."

Pastor Roy looked at me seriously, but a little smile crept over his face. "Pastor Max, you're going to be with me." It was all that needed to be said. Though I didn't have a place in the pack of surfers at Makaha, Pastor Roy did. The implication was clear: he would validate my place and he would be my cover. I would have a place in the pack not because of anything I had done or could do, but solely because of who Pastor Roy was and what he was willing to do for me.

In many ways that is a simple illustration of grace, the love freely given as a result of unmerited favor. Grace between friends is sweet, but it is only a small hint of the powerful grace of God available to us in Jesus Christ. Pastor Roy knows a good deal about that grace as well.

After a challenging childhood in what he describes as a "very violent upbringing," Roy found his way into a bad crowd in one of the rough neighborhoods of Oahu. Illegal drug use became the focal point of his life, and by the time he was in his twenties, this former college football lineman had moved from a promising future to a thousand-dollar-a-day drug habit which he supported by getting criminally involved with a local drug syndicate. Roy's criminal activities ran the gamut: assault, kidnapping, extortion, attempted murder, and second-degree robbery. After multiple arrests, he finally hit bottom. Incarcerated and facing several serious charges that carried a sentence of up to eighty years in prison, Roy began to despair. Depression weighed on his soul. He thought of ending his life. In many ways, he was echoing the cry of Isaiah when his life was exposed: "I am ruined!" (Isa. 6:5a).

Roy's cellmate, a Christ-follower, invited Roy to a prison Bible study. When some of his former partners in crime saw Roy walking through the prison with a Bible, they mocked him. He softly said, "My lawyer can't help me out of this. You can't help me. Let's see what God can do for me." At that Bible study the young prisoner encountered the grace of God in Christ Jesus for the first time. Later, in his four-foot-by-eight-foot cell that could potentially be his home for the next eighty years, Roy knelt and said one of the most honest prayers any of us can ever pray: "Help me, Jesus." In doing so, he discovered the grace of God. Roy knew immediately: "I was a new person when I said that prayer." He was absolutely right. He had said a prayer God always answers!

Through an amazing series of legal proceedings, a Christian judge saw potential in Roy and dropped the charges against him. He was released from prison in 1996. But in 1998, Roy's case was appealed again. He appeared in court and pled guilty. But this time, Roy wasn't alone. Dozens of members of the church he attended came to support him, testifying that he was a new person. The judge was so impressed that he cut Roy free from serving any additional time.

In gratitude for all the Lord had done for him, Roy launched a ministry called Camp Agape that ministers to the children of prisoners in Hawaii. And in a twist that seemingly only God could orchestrate, both of the judges who presided over his court hearings and decided to give him freedom work alongside Roy in Camp Agape. They have all become not only brothers in Christ, but dear friends.

Time and again over the ensuing twenty-one years since the second hearing that freed him for good, Pastor Roy has turned to Psalm 91, the entirety of which he sees as his story. The last verse sums up his testimony: "He will call on me, and I will answer him" (v. 15a).

Isaiah Looks Outward

Even as Isaiah is crying out that he is "ruined" (Isa. 6:5), his gaze moves from the inward look at his personal state to the outward look, where he discovers his source of help. It is in that place of complete brokenness, when we are at the end of ourselves, and understand completely our utter dependence on help from outside that God does His best work. There we see the grace of God.

The scripture says that as Isaiah cried out, "one of the seraphim flew to me with a live coal in his hand, which he had taken with tongs from the altar. With it he touched my mouth and said, 'See, this has touched your lips; your guilt it taken away and your sin is atoned for'" (vv. 6–7).

In Isaiah's day, atonement had to do with the cleansing of impurity, within the priesthood, among the people and within the nation of Israel. There were rigorous laws and rituals around atonement, all designed to ensure the purity and cleanness of the people of God so that God would not remove His presence from the temple. In this instance, however, Isaiah does nothing to "atone" for his sins. He has recognized his need, but that is all. He performs no rituals, pays no price, and even says no prayers. He is simply pronounced clean. His guilt is pronounced removed and his sin atoned for. How is this possible?

In order to get a clear understanding of what is happening here, it is important to answer a fundamental question: When the scripture says that Isaiah "saw the Lord . . . seated on a throne" (v. 1), who is it that Isaiah saw? The text says, "the Lord," of course, but who is "the Lord"? This side of the cross, we know the answer. The earliest claim of the church and her believers is that Jesus is Lord. Jesus is Lord to the glory of God the Father. Of course, Isaiah lived long before Jesus walked on the earth. There is great mystery in this passage. Things become clearer, however, when we look at some important truths Scripture reveals concerning seeing God. When Moses had his personal encounters with God, he was forced to hide and to avert his gaze. God said to Moses, "you cannot see my face, for no one may see me and live" (Ex. 33:20). Isaiah, of course, knew these words well.

The apostle John, however, adds some further light: "No one has ever seen God, but the one and only Son, who is himself God and is in closest relationship with the Father, has made him known" (John 1:18). John tells us that only Jesus, the Son of God, has ever seen God. Yet, Jesus has made Him known. To see Jesus is to see the Lord. Jesus is Lord.

Isaiah had a phenomenal gift given to him. God peeled back the heavens and showed Isaiah our glorified King of kings, seated on the throne. Some might say at this point, "I simply don't believe that. Surely Isaiah lived long before the days of Jesus." Skepticism around claims such as these is always healthy. But again, the apostle John helps us: "Isaiah said this [Isaiah 6] because he saw Jesus' glory and spoke about him" (John 12:41).

The seraph could take those tongs from that altar, touch Isaiah's lips, and declare that Isaiah's sin was cleansed and his life had been atoned, because the Son of God was seated on that throne. The fact that the Lord was seated on the throne is important. When did Jesus sit on the throne? According to Scripture it was when He uttered, "It is finished" (John 19:30). Hebrews captures it beautifully: "The Son is the radiance of God's glory and the exact representation of his being, sustaining all things by his powerful word. After he had provided purification for sins, he sat down at the right hand of the Majesty in heaven" (Heb. 1:3).

Later, Hebrews says: "Day after day every priest stands and performs his religious duties; again and again he offers the same sacrifices, which can never take away sins. But when this priest had offered for all time one sacrifice for sins, he sat down at the right hand of God" (10:11–12). The earthly priests, day after day after day after day, are offering these earthly sacrifices one after another early in the morning, late in the afternoon, then early the next morning and late the next afternoon. The blood is flowing. But there is one huge problem: all this sacrifice can't do a thing about the people's sin, individually or collectively. However, when this Priest (Jesus) had offered for all time one sacrifice for sin, He sat down at the right hand of God. It was finished. He sat on the throne. The sacrificial system was finished. The price was paid in full. There was no need for further sacrifice.

What was it that made Isaiah's lips pure? It was certainly not anything Isaiah did. Nor was it anything he said. It was not even his willingness to follow the Lord. Isaiah had made no move to follow anyone. In fact, it was not about anything in Isaiah's life. Instead, it was entirely because the Lord, in His grace, His mercy, His forethought, His sacrifice on the cross, that one substitutionary sacrifice that made the difference for everyone, having atoned for his sins, touched him, cleansed him, and said to him, "You are clean!"

My Identity in Jesus

One of the things I love about Isaiah is that during this remarkable encounter with the Lord, he doesn't argue with the angels, nor with God. Having just become intimately aware of the depths of his own sinfulness, Isaiah is suddenly pronounced clean by a hot-coal-wielding seraph, and he seemingly accepts that statement at face value. Isaiah doesn't list all the reasons why he couldn't possibly be clean. He doesn't try to negotiate the price. He doesn't question how this could happen. He simply accepts that he is who God says he is.

Additionally, Isaiah appears to believe that something essential and transformative has happened to him. The book of Isaiah is one of the longest in the Bible, and this episode comes near the beginning. There is no doubt that Isaiah's life had its ups and downs following this moment of forgiveness, yet we never read of Isaiah coming back to the Lord saying, "Lord, could you round up those seraphim again, and get that coal cooker going, I'm going to need another cleansing. I don't think you got the job done the last time." Isaiah models for us how to accept our identity in Christ.

The gospel of John tells us: "Yet to all who did receive him, to those who believed in his name, he gave the right to become children of God" (John 1:12). Because of the atonement of Christ, we are by faith adopted into the family of God. Jesus later says, "So if the Son sets you free, you will be free indeed" (John 8:36). Speaking about this freedom and adoption we have in Jesus, the apostle Paul says to the Romans: "For I am convinced that neither death nor life, neither angels nor demons, neither the present nor the future, nor any powers, neither height nor depth, nor anything else in all creation, will be able to separate us from the love of God that is in Christ Jesus our Lord" (8:38–39).

I was blessed to be part of a church that performed scores of adult baptisms every month. It was literally wonderful to see all of those women and men making a public profession of their faith, and sealing it by following Jesus in baptism. As they were spiritually buried with Christ and raised to new life with Him (see Romans 6:4), we could often see the transformation taking place right before our eyes. The joy and mystery and wonder of it all was palpable. Yet one aspect of those services always concerned me. There were a few people (not many) who would show up on a regular basis wanting to be baptized again and again. I finally asked one young man, "Brother, how many times do you think God has to adopt you before it takes?" The issue was not needing to be rebaptized. If God is the main actor in baptism (and He is), then showing up for a do-over suggests that somehow God wasn't up to the task the first time. And we all know that idea is absurd. The issue was, instead, a failure to accept a new identity in Jesus. Sometimes I need to accept that I am a child of God because God says I am, regardless of how I feel.

Of course, God is concerned about our purity and holiness. God desires to break the power of sin in our lives, to cleanse us of our sins, to fill us with His glory, and to move us from glory to glory until the image of God is restored in our lives. But that is a process that God works, through the power of the Holy Spirit, in the lives of those who abide in Him and draw close to Him and the means of grace. It is not something a believer always feels, nor is it something we try to do on our own.

Holiness of life is vitally important, but at times the church has watered holiness down to a list of rules and regulations—the dos and don'ts of holy living. When I was a boy, people in Kentucky would often say the holiness people were those who "don't smoke, don't drink, and don't chew . . . and don't go out with girls who do." Sadly, when holiness is equated with a list of dos and don'ts, it often becomes more about who controls the lists or how believers can doctor up their exterior lives to give an appearance of being holy. This rules-oriented holiness also causes many people to stumble. If they fail at something on this list, they begin to believe that either they are not children of God after all, or that they need to get saved again.

Jesus, however, said, "What goes into someone's mouth does not defile them, but what comes out of their mouth, that is what defiles them" (Matt. 15:11). He was letting us know that holiness is an internal process, and begins in the heart. It is the work of God.

The recipients of grace are drawn to that work because Jesus, the source of that grace (and the peace, freedom, and love that accompany it) is now their Lord. His burden is light, His yoke is easy (see Matthew 11:30), and He is capable of doing His work in the hearts of all who remain in Him. This work is what sanctification is all about. In the meantime, we have the assurance from the apostle Paul that "the Spirit himself testifies with our spirit that we are God's children" (Rom. 8:16). When that assurance of the Holy Spirit is present in our hearts, we can be confident in our identity in Jesus.

That is the good news. That's the way it works for every one of us. Isaiah was given a preview of God's salvation story for humanity. In his moment of need he looked outward and saw and experienced the grace of God in Jesus Christ. The very grace of God inspired John Newton to write the great hymn "Amazing Grace," and inspires the world to continue to sing it with joy and conviction.

> Amazing grace! How sweet the sound
> That saved a wretch like me!
> I once was lost, but now am found;
> Was blind, but now I see.
>
> 'Twas grace that taught my heart to fear,
> and grace my fears relieved;
> how precious did that grace appear
> the hour I first believed!
>
> Through many dangers, toils and snares,
> I have already come;
> 'Tis grace hath brought me safe thus far,
> And grace will lead me home.
>
> The Lord has promised good to me,

His Word my hope secures;
He will my Shield and Portion be,
As long as life endures.

Yea, when this flesh and heart shall fail,
And mortal life shall cease,
I shall possess, within the veil,
A life of joy and peace.

The earth shall soon dissolve like snow,
The sun forbear to shine;
But God, who called me here below,
Will be forever mine.[1]

This grace is available to every human being for the asking. The only thing we bring is an understanding of our need and a desire to receive it. And, even more amazingly, we will discover that it has been God all along, drawing us to the point of knowing our need, and wooing us to Himself, so that He might share with us His deep love for us.

Amazing Grace

Although the grace of God is about what the Lord does, not what we do, there are discernable movements in the life of grace. John Wesley and those in the early Wesleyan movement came up with a coherent way to speak about the various ways God's grace operates in our lives. They articulated three movements of grace.

Grace is not something God does; it is an essential aspect of who God is. Wherever God in His glory is present, grace is flowing, and as we know from

---

1. John Newton, "Amazing Grace," 1779. Public domain.

the seraphim's song, "the whole earth is full of his glory" (Isa. 6:3b), Wesley referred to this ever-present, universal grace as "prevenient" grace. *Prevenient*, a word derived from Latin, simply means "that which goes before." Prevenient grace means the grace of God that is around us all, and at work in everyone, even before we know or care about it.

In his message "The Scripture Way of Salvation," Wesley wrote that prevenient grace is "all that is wrought in the soul by what is frequently termed 'natural conscience,' . . . that 'light' wherewith the Son of God 'enlighteneth everyone that cometh into the world.'"[2] It is God going before us, wooing us to Himself. It is the residual, tarnished image of God that still remains in each of us. It is our conscience that tells us that right and wrong exist and nags at our hearts when we move against it. Indeed, Wesley asserts that we would not even be able to utter the name of God were it not for the Lord's gracious going before, calling out to us, seeking us, and putting His name on our lips.

God is a missionary God, as evidenced by His willingness to seek Adam and Eve out despite their sin, shame, and hiding in the garden. The Lord's prevenient grace is on full display as He calls to them, encouraging them to come out of the darkness of their hiding and return to His light. The apostle John tells us that, in Jesus Christ, God continues this missionary work: "The true light that gives light to everyone was coming

---

2. John Wesley, *The Works of John Wesley*, ed. Albert C. Outler, Sermon 43, "The Scripture Way of Salvation" (Nashville, TN: Abingdon Press, 1984–2015).

into the world" (John 1:9). Note that Jesus gives light to everyone!

All my life I have heard testimonies of people who tell of how they found the Lord. And though I know exactly what they mean, it is, nonetheless, a false assertion. They were no more looking for the Lord than were Adam and Eve in the garden. It is God who comes looking for us, offering His grace, and wooing us to His love. At best, we can say we have been found by God. Isaiah may have turned his eyes heavenward, but the Lord came to him. God sought Pastor Roy out in that prison cell, and God is seeking all of us in the same way, and He has been doing so since the moment we were formed in our mothers' wombs.

There is a second expression of grace that Wesley referred to as "justifying" grace. A Sunday school teacher explained to me as a nine-year-old that "justification" meant "just as if I never sinned." And while his definition may be a bit of an oversimplification, it gets at the heart of the matter. Justification is concerned with pardon. It is the forgiveness of our sins, but also our complete acceptance by God, our adoption as children of God, and our rightful place in the kingdom of God. We talked in the last chapter about repentance being a turning away from sin and toward the Lord. Justifying grace includes the assurance in our spirit that we are, indeed, accepted and welcomed by the one toward whom we have turned in that repentance. It allows our hearts to believe that the atonement of Jesus was sufficient for our forgiveness and cleansing, and to embrace our new identity as forgiven, chosen, children of God.

"Sanctifying" grace is God's coming to us in our forgiveness, and through the power of the Holy Spirit, working to restore the fullness of the image of God in which we were created. Wesley also affirmed that God's grace seeks nothing less than a new creation in the image of Jesus Christ. The apostle Paul spoke of this process of sanctification as moving from glory to glory into the very image of Christ (see 2 Corinthians 3:18). We will speak more about sanctifying grace in the following chapters.

"Who Do You Say That I Am?"

As Jesus was walking along the road to Caesarea Philippi with His disciples one day, He asked them, "Who do you say that I am?" It was an important question, and still is. Peter got it right when he declared: "You are the Christ, the Son of the Living God." Jesus assured him that not only was he correct, but that even his answer was a product of God's grace. "Flesh and blood didn't reveal this to you," Jesus told him, "but my Father in heaven" (see Matthew 16:13–17). The Lord is still asking people that same question today. But this side of the cross, a second, equally important question comes to those who answer as Peter did: Do you accept that you are who I say that you are?

One of the greatest challenges that any believer faces is simply to believe that we are who the Lord says we are. In that moment of brokenness when we come to the foot of the cross and cry out to the Lord and God says, "Your guilt is taken away and your sins are atoned for," do we have faith to accept Him at His word? It is often difficult for us to do so, and we have many internal objections.

We say, "But I don't feel like I am cleansed!" It doesn't matter. We say, "But I still have sin in my life!" It doesn't matter. Remember, God already knows exactly who we are and everything that we have ever thought, said, or done. Can we trust that we are who Jesus says we are?

A lot of people have developed a mistaken impression of who Jesus is. We have this idea of a judgmental, disciplinarian Jesus who is going around looking for everything we do wrong. As if our Lord is some sort of cosmic hall monitor who is out to get us. But that's not the Lord we follow. The apostle Paul says, "Therefore, there is now no condemnation for those who are in Christ Jesus" (Rom. 8:1). The Lord gives us a clean slate. Yes, He wants us to move forward in holiness, and He will lead us there if we cooperate with His Spirit, but grace allows us to start with a clean slate and total forgiveness.

Paul tells the church at Corinth: "Therefore, if anyone is in Christ, he is a new creation; old things have passed away, and look, new things have come" (2 Cor. 5:17 HCSB). We are spiritually born again. We start over.

I remember hearing a revival preacher many years ago say, "You need to understand that the Christian life is like a man who owned two bulldogs. The dogs represent the 'old self' and the 'new self.' The idea is that they are fighting for domination over the man's life. So, what we need to do is feed the 'new self' and starve the 'old self' because the one that is going to prevail is the one you feed!"

Maybe you have heard this illustration as well. Maybe it has even made sense to you. Sadly, it is a contradiction of 2 Corinthians 5:17. According to Paul, when we are in Christ, the old has "passed away." Here's a thought: If you have a live bulldog and a dead bulldog, what difference does it make whether or not you keep feeding the dead one? Granted, it is a complete waste of time and resources, and you will get nothing in return, but the dead dog is not coming back to life. And to live as if it is coming back to life is simply a waste of the new life you've been given in Jesus.

Receiving the Lord's justifying grace is about trusting that when we come, broken, at the foot of the cross, those seraphim are able to touch us in the same was they touched Isaiah. And we can and will become who and what Jesus says we are. We will not only be a new creation, we will also no longer have condemnation.

> The Spirit you received does not make you slaves, so that you live in fear again; rather, the Spirit you received brought about your adoption to sonship. And by him we cry, *"Abba,* Father."* The Spirit himself testifies with our spirit that we are God's children. Now if we are children, then we are heirs—heirs of God and co-heirs with Christ, if indeed we share in his sufferings in order that we may also share in his glory. (Rom. 8:15–17)

We are not only children of God, we are joint heirs of the kingdom of God! Sadly, many believers are moping around, saying, "I'm just a poor sinner saved by grace." Look, all of us are poor sinners, and we most assuredly have been saved by grace. But we are so much more as well. Our identity in Christ is as conquerors; in fact, more than conquerors. Look at what Peter, a man well-acquainted with sin and even denial of the Lord, says:

> But you are a chosen people, a royal priest-hood, a holy nation, God's special possession, that you may declare the praises of him who called you out of darkness into his wonderful light. Once you were not a people, but now you are the people of God; once you had not received mercy, but now you have received mercy. (1 Peter 2:9–10)

Isaiah says the whole temple was filled with the glory of God. But this side of the cross, the temple on earth has been destroyed and now those who have been given new life in Jesus are the temple of God. Our bodies are the temple of God, and Scripture says where He dwells, there the whole temple is filled with the glory of God (see Exodus 40:34–35; Ezekiel 43:5; 44:4; Haggai 2:7; 2 Chronicles 7:1–2). If our very beings are filled with the glory of God, this truth has massive implications about not only how we live, but also about how we see ourselves and how we carry ourselves in this world. Some of us need to begin to believe and accept that we are who the Lord says that we are.

We do have an enemy, however, and he is a liar! Satan does not want us to believe that we are who the Lord says we are. He is, after all, hell-bent on our destruction. I believe the most dangerous word in the Enemy's arsenal is the word *if*. Consider the baptism of Jesus. The Lord went down to John at the Jordan and John, at first, was put off. "It is I who should be baptized by you," John says. But Jesus says, "Let's let it happen the way the Scriptures say that it should." Jesus humbles Himself for the baptism, and when

He comes up out of the water, the heavens open up, the Holy Spirit descends like a dove, and a voice from heaven booms out saying, "This is my beloved Son, and I am pleased with Him!" It feels awkward thinking of that same thing happening at our baptisms, but in a very real spiritual sense, the Bible says that it does. In Jesus' case, this is an amazing moment. God leaves no doubt about who Jesus is: "My beloved Son" (see Matthew 3:13–17 HCSB). God expresses His absolute pleasure in Jesus.

The thing I always find most incredible, however, is what happens next. With these words of His heavenly Father still ringing in His ears, Jesus is driven by the Holy Spirit into the wilderness alone. The very next word He hears comes from Satan: "If." Satan says, "If you are the Son of God . . ." It doesn't matter much what words come next. The most serious challenge Satan is presenting to Jesus is to try to make Jesus doubt His relationship with His heavenly Father. Remember, the last words Jesus had heard were His Father saying, "This is My beloved Son . . . " Now Satan believes that he can sow doubt into Jesus' mind on this essential question. Of course, Satan was unsuccessful with Jesus in this regard. But here is the point: If Satan thought he could pull that one off with Jesus, don't you know that he believes he can pull it off with us as well?

God says we are adopted into His family, joint heirs with Jesus to the kingdom, a chosen race, a royal priesthood, a holy nation, His own special set apart people. He assures us we are forgiven, cleansed, accepted, and set free. But the moment any of us receive the grace of God, Satan comes along almost immediately and says, "Whoa, wait a minute. If you were really all those things you wouldn't act like you do. You wouldn't say the things you say. You wouldn't think the things you think." And sometimes the Enemy succeeds in discouraging us in this way, getting us to doubt whether we really are who the Lord says we are. Then, we sometimes try to make ourselves more religious, to follow more rules, to dress ourselves up as holy. And when we believe that our thoughts or actions disqualify us from God's grace, we can even begin to live in shame and return to hiding our true selves from God once again, the very state from which He has rescued us in the first place.

I don't believe that the kingdom of God will ever advance on this earth in the way that God intends for it to advance until God's people, the recipients of His grace, begin to believe that they are who He says they are, and to live their lives in accordance with His declaration of who and Whose they are.

There is a beautiful story from the days of John F. Kennedy's presidency. As with all administrations, there was strict security around the Oval Office in the White House. Several layers of security were required for anyone who would enter. There were strict protocols in place for how, when, and in what way individuals were allowed to engage with the president. One foreign diplomat was surprised, therefore, when visiting the president, to note a small boy casually walking past all the security points outside the Oval Office. The child burst in the door, walked quickly past everyone in the room, hugged the president's waist, and then disappeared under the desk at the president's feet. It was, of course, John-John, the president's son. John Kennedy had given strict instructions during his presidency that no one was ever to obstruct his son's access to his father. As the son of the president, John-John had unrestricted access to his father, and his father's love.

If it is true that it is good to be the king, sometimes it is even better to be the child of the king. In the grace of our Lord, we who are children of the King have been given unhindered access to the throne room and the Father! And with it, to the Father's love.

I walk differently when I know I am a child of the King. I walk differently when I believe that one day I will reign together with Jesus in His kingdom. I walk differently when I understand that I am part of the group Jesus referred to saying, "You didn't choose me; I chose you! And I chose you to go forth and bear fruit, fruit that will remain!" (see John 15:16). I walk differently when I believe that Jesus meant it when He said, "You will do even greater things than I have done in My name!" (see John 14:12).

Jesus did it. He did it all. He paid the price. He earned our forgiveness. He is the author and perfecter of our faith (see Hebrews 12:2). He is our advocate (see 1 John 2:1) and defender before the Father. He is the source of our abundant life in this world and our lives with Him for eternity. It is *all* about Jesus. That is why when we look outward, we receive His grace and we fix our eyes on Him.

At Home with the Lord

Many years ago, someone told me of a survey that revealed three phrases that people most long to hear at home. It turned out they were all important indicators of a happy, healthy home where those present are loved and accepted. What most everyone needed to hear was:

"I love you."

"I forgive you."

"Dinner's ready."

In very many ways, the grace of God is about finding an eternal home where all three are heard. The scripture says, "But God demonstrates his own love for us in this: While we were still sinners, Christ died for us" (Rom. 5:8). God went to unmeasurable lengths to demonstrate His love for us. On the cross, our Savior, the atonement for our sins said, "Father, forgive them, for they do not know what they are doing" (Luke 23:34). With His last breath, the Lord says, "I forgive you." All of this opened us up to the possibilities of life in the kingdom. In some of the final words of Jesus recorded in Scripture, He says, "Here I am! I stand at the door and knock. If anyone hears my voice and opens the door, I will come in and eat with that person, and they with me" (Rev. 3:20). We are loved. We are forgiven. Dinner's ready. You've been invited to dine with the King.

The Lord looks to each of us, inviting us to join Him in His kingdom. He goes before us, preparing the way, wooing us to Himself. And He invites us into the abundant life that only He can give. And when we protest our unworthiness, our unfitness, and our sense that perhaps others are better suited and more qualified for that life than we, He says to us what Pastor Roy said to me about Makaha: "You are going to be with me!" Because of His amazing grace, that is always all that needs to be said.

SIX

Free to Live

"Then neither do I condemn you," Jesus declared. "Go now and leave your life of sin."

—JOHN 8:11B

Yes, grace is the unmerited favor of God, but it is also inextricably linked to the holy love of God. Indeed, grace is the tangible expression of God's holy love. Legalism and judgmentalism, on the other hand, are deeply at odds with God's grace. It isn't that grace is opposed to the law; far from it. According to Paul: "No one will be declared righteous in God's sight by the works of the law; rather, through the law we become conscious of our sin" (Rom. 3:20). The law serves to bring about awareness or consciousness of sin. Legalism seeks to wield the law as a cudgel, bringing sin to light in order to cleanse the world of both sin and sinners. It seeks to condemn and to destroy. And it is often discriminatory and capricious in its application. Grace, on the other hand, seeks to work with the law in response to awareness of sin, evil, and brokenness with an aim toward the destruction of the power of sin and the redemption of the sinner. Perhaps nowhere is this more evident than in the story of Jesus' encounter with the woman caught in adultery.

The Feast of Tabernacles has just finished, and the next day dawns to find Jesus seated in the temple ministering to some of the remaining crowd of pilgrims. The Lord's teaching is suddenly interrupted by a group of religious leaders, teachers of the law, and Pharisees (a particularly legalistic sect of Judaism). In their custody is a disheveled woman who is flung unceremoniously at the feet of Jesus, accused by these men of being caught in the act of adultery. The Pharisees ask Jesus what should be done with the woman, given that the law says that one caught in the act of adultery should be put to death by stoning.

There are immediate questions that arise in this scenario and none of them would have been lost on Jesus. The law did, indeed, specify stoning for those caught in the act of adultery: "If a man commits adultery with another man's wife—with the wife of his neighbor—both the adulterer and the adulteress are to be put to death" (Lev. 20:10). Note that both the man and the woman were subject to death. According to the accusers, the woman was caught in the act. That obviously necessitates the presence of a man as well. Yet the man involved is nowhere to be seen. Right away, this suggests that far from a concern for the moral purity of the community, these religious leaders are using the woman and her sin (and the law) as pawns in a more nefarious scheme.

Additionally, according to the law, in order for this woman to be charged with adultery, the act itself had to have been personally witnessed by two non-participatory men. It seems odd that there could have been two eyewitnesses unless the whole episode was part of a setup, perhaps even by the religious leaders themselves. Some have speculated that the absence of the man may indicate that the man was also a Pharisee or a teacher of the law himself, and a part of this whole plot to discredit Jesus. There is no way to know for sure. But clearly, those committed to full enforcement of the letter of the law should have had the man present as well.

Finally, according to the law, the witnesses bringing the accusation were, upon conviction, to throw the first stones. This was supposed to help ensure the veracity of the witnesses. The law was clear: this woman caught in the act of adultery should be stoned. Yet these experts in the law had brought her to Jesus asking what should be done with her. Clearly, they did not have a legal conundrum. They knew as well as Jesus what the law said. Instead, they were trying to publicly point out Jesus' disrespect (in their opinion) for the law, with all of His talk of love, mercy, and forgiveness. Grace often creates a negative response in those bound to legalism.

Jesus' initial reaction is fascinating. Still seated in His teaching position, the Lord leans over and begins to doodle in the dust of the temple floor. What He wrote in the dirt is forever lost to history. But one thing is certain, Jesus' lack of an immediate response sends a message to these pompous religious leaders that He is not beholden to them. And while we can only speculate what Jesus may have written, since ancient times many have suggested that it may have been Jeremiah 17:13: "LORD, you are the hope of Israel; all who forsake you will be put to shame. Those who turn away from you will be written in the dust because they have forsaken the LORD, the spring of living water." Even if this was not what Jesus wrote, the words were certainly fitting for the occasion.

Anyone who has ever tried to simply ignore self-righteous zealots knows that this usually only serves to enrage them. Such was the case with the Pharisees, who kept pressing Jesus until He finally straightened up and said, in essence: "I think you ought to stone her. Put her to death. The law is clear. But before you go into action, I have this one small requirement: 'Let any one of you who is without sin be the first to throw a stone at her'" (see John 8:7). Then Jesus bent back down and went back to doodling in the dirt. I heard an evangelist say that he guessed Jesus was writing the names of the girlfriends of the Pharisees and teachers of the law!

Remember that the law said the accusers should throw the first stones. But did they really want to be under the scrutiny of the crowd, and the Lord, in saying they were not guilty of violations of the law themselves? Likely, they had been complicit in the setup from the start. Certainly, they had failed to bring the man along as the law required. And the law was very specific in its harshness toward anyone who would bear false witness.

There are some scholars who have suggested that Jesus' words could be accurately read as: "Let any one of you who is without this sin be the first to throw a stone at her." After all, Jesus had redefined adultery in the Sermon on the Mount: "You have heard that it was said, 'You shall not commit adultery.' But I tell you that anyone who looks at a woman lustfully has already committed adultery with her in his heart" (Matt. 5:27–28). Was it likely that there were any there who had never lusted in their hearts, who had never dealt with impure thoughts? Whatever the case, according to the Bible, one by one, beginning with the eldest, they put down their stones and went home, all while Jesus ignored them and continued to draw in the dust.

It is critical to note that at no point in this encounter did Jesus denigrate the law or deny its force. He simply took the law out of a specific application and applied it justly across all people. He suggested that those who would judge should apply the law to their own hearts first, before seeking to hand out penalties to others. It was also in the Sermon on the Mount that Jesus said about judgment: "Do not judge, or you too will be judged" (Matt. 7:1). Nor is Jesus in any way suggesting that sin is not important; He will deal with that issue with the woman herself.

What Jesus is doing, however, is calling into question a form of outward holiness that is more concerned with appearance that cleanliness of heart. He is challenging a letter of the law of legalism that tends to use the law and power to its own twisted ends rather than for the good purposes for which it was given. Jesus notes the savage delight these pious legalists have in catching the woman in their trap. He detects their pompous pride in being able to use her as a pawn in their plans. He has already been the recipient of their vengeful anger that drives them to oppose Him. And by the time chapter 8 of John's gospel ends, this same crowd of Pharisees and teachers of the law will be attempting to stone Jesus. There is nothing quite so dangerous as a legalist scorned.

The Grace of Life

Once the religious crowd has departed, the scene narrows to only the woman and Jesus. The original crowd of people to whom Jesus had been speaking may still have been present, but it is apparent that Jesus' whole focus is on the woman. Jesus again straightens up from His temple floor art project and asks her: "Woman, where are they? Has no one condemned you?" (John 8:10). Her response is interesting. As she looks into the loving eyes of Jesus, she must sense what is about to come, because He has asked her if anyone condemns her. He is the teacher, the one many are already calling Messiah. She had to know that although the others had all dropped their stones and left, she still faced one who could condemn her. And He could do so even by the rules He had just put in place; He was the one person there who was without sin. Yet, she simply responds, "No one, sir" (v. 11a).

I have often wondered how she said those words. The tone and emotion of her response. Was she unnerved, mystified, elated, ashamed, relieved, hopeful, or terrified? Was she possibly some combination of all of those emotions and many others all at the same time? It is not possible to know. But this woman who, moments earlier, had been facing the prospect of a death sentence for a crime in which she had been justly caught was about to experience the grace of God in full. Jesus said to her, "Then neither do I condemn you. . . . Go now and leave your life of sin" (v. 11b).

Through the centuries, many have commented on this story with concern that there is no evidence the woman asked for forgiveness. There is no outward expression of confession or remorse. Some are troubled that, by offering these words of grace, Jesus is condoning her sin, even giving permission to sin. They are bothered by how seemingly undeserved it all appears. But that is the nature of grace. By definition, it is always undeserved. It would be wrong, however, to assume that by offering grace Jesus was encouraging or even condoning her sin.

Grace, the unmerited favor of God, seeks to break the power of sin. Because Jesus has come to bring life—abundant life (see John 10:10)—and sin is antithetical to that life, He is absolutely concerned about sin and about her particular sin. Not because it is a violation of the rules, but because it is an impediment to the life she was created to live, the life that is available to her in Jesus. But if her sin was blocking her from receiving that life, it was also holding her in bondage to itself. There is an important truth at play here: it is only on the backside of grace that we can say to someone, "Go, and leave your life of sin."

The apostle Paul was well aware of this reality. In Romans he speaks of his own bondage to sin:

> We know that the law is spiritual; but I am unspiritual, sold as a slave to sin. I do not understand what I do. For what I want to do I do not do, but what I hate I do. And if I do what I do not want to do, I agree that the law is good. As it is, it is no longer I myself who do it, but it is sin living in me. For I know that good itself does not dwell in me, that is, in my sinful nature. For I have the desire to do what is good, but I cannot carry it out. For I do not do the good I want to do, but the evil I do not want to do—this I keep on doing. Now

> if I do what I do not want to do, it is no longer
> I who do it, but it is sin living in me that does
> it. (Rom. 7:14–20)

You can see the war going on in Paul's very soul,
just as it goes on in the soul of everyone who is in
bondage to sin. But then Paul wraps up by saying:

> Thanks be to God, who delivers me through
> Jesus Christ our Lord! So then, I myself in my
> mind am a slave to God's law, but in my sinful
> nature a slave to the law of sin. Therefore, there
> is now no condemnation for those who are in
> Christ Jesus, because through Christ Jesus the
> law of the Spirit who gives life has set you free
> from the law of sin and death. (Rom. 7:25–8:2)

It is the grace of our Lord, who refuses to condemn
us though He has every right to do so, that breaks the
bondage of sin in our lives. It opens us up to the possibilities of the life Jesus longs to give us.

The Nature of Grace

Grace does not negate the law; instead, it helps bring
about the fulfillment of the law. Jesus was asked by a
Pharisee one day to name the greatest commandment
in the law. He did not limit it to one, but instead spoke
of two, inextricably linked together: "'Love the Lord
your God with all your heart and with all your soul
and with all your mind.' This is the first and greatest
commandment. And the second is like it: 'Love your
neighbor as yourself.' All the Law and the Prophets
hang on these two commandments" (Matt. 22:37–40).
These words of Jesus have come to be known as the

"Great Commandment." It is the law of love. Jesus says the point of it all is to love the Lord with everything we have and to love others in the same way. In doing so, Jesus says, we have reached the pinnacle of the law.

Love is always expressed in relationship. When the Lord brings His grace to bear in our lives, it is always concerned with deepening and strengthening our relationship with Him. Love values being in right relationship even more than being right. It is always outwardly focused and always seeks the best for the other. When Jesus brings His loving grace to bear on the woman caught in adultery, He is concerned with how to bring her into closer relationship with God and with others, and how to usher her into life. In so doing, He is helping her to move toward fulfilling the highest purpose of the law. He is also helping her move toward the abundant life that He came to bring.

Grace is free, but it is not cheap. The reason the Lord is able to so freely bring His grace to bear with the woman caught in adultery is precisely because He knows that He is going to take the price of her sin upon Himself. Grace pays the price. True love is always sacrificial, and grace is the embodiment of God's sacrificial love.

John 3:16, the verse Martin Luther called "the gospel in miniature," is a well-known declaration of the gospel of love: "For God so loved the world that he gave his one and only Son, that whoever believes in him shall not perish but have eternal life." Sometimes we forget the verse that follows: "For God did not send his Son into the world to condemn the world, but to save the world through him" (v. 17). Grace is about life, salvation, and redemption, but never about condemnation.

Grace goes first, because that's what love does. Remember that Scripture says while we were still sinners Jesus went to the cross (see Romans 5:8). Jesus understood that love goes first. God's prevenient grace draws us to the Lord when we would not otherwise even be mindful of Him. God's justifying grace comes while we are still caught, like the woman in the story, guilty and deserving death. Then, when our redemption creates in us a desire to live a holy and obedient life (as it always does), God's sanctifying grace goes first, and begins its work of breaking the power of sin in our lives and cleansing us from all unrighteousness.

Sanctifying Grace

Jesus said to the woman caught in adultery, "Go now and leave your life of sin" (John 8:11b). To be honest, that would be a somewhat ungracious thing to say if this woman was on her own to try to overcome the power of sin in her life. She had already shown an inability to do so. "Try harder," does not seem to be gracious or helpful counsel. But Jesus is aware of an aspect of grace that changes the equation. The Lord in His gracious love gives us sanctifying grace.

Just as God goes before us with His prevenient grace—wooing us to Himself and His love—and cleanses us with His justifying grace—changing our relationship and refusing to condemn us—the Lord begins His work in us with His sanctifying grace—breaking the power of sin in our lives and beginning the process of moving us from glory to glory into the image of Jesus (see 2 Corinthians 3:18). He is literally restoring the image of God in us.

Again, John Wesley is helpful in understanding the work of sanctifying grace. In his message "Justification by Faith," Wesley assures us that sanctification is the immediate fruit of justification. The moment we experience God's acceptance and adoption through justifying grace (and are given a fresh start, or "born again"), the Lord also imparts the Holy Spirit to begin His sanctifying work in our lives. This is such powerful good news because, as Paul pointed out earlier, without the help of the Lord, we would be utterly defenseless against the power of sin.

There are two types of grace available in the life of faith: free grace and cooperative grace. Free grace is given to us out of God's abundant love and because of God's own good pleasure. Creation and life itself are examples of free grace. We did not participate in any way in either creation or our own life. Cooperative grace is also freely given. But its efficacy in our lives is largely determined by our willingness to actively cooperate with the Holy Spirit in the work He is doing in our lives. Sanctifying grace works that way. God graciously gives us a way to break the power of sin in our lives and offers us the opportunity to cooperate with Him in making us holy. As we abide in Him in an ongoing way, we are perfected in love and made more and more like Him.

I have contended throughout this book that the focus of our gaze determines the state of our being. There is a corollary that modern-day psychologists and sociologists have long understood as well. People tend to become like what the most significant voices in their lives communicate to them that they are. This truth plays out in all areas of our lives. People who

constantly hear voices of condemnation and criti-
cism from the significant voices in their lives tend to
become beaten down and broken. People who hear
encouraging voices that communicate in ways that
value them and their contribution to the world tend to
excel and feel good about themselves. In our day-to-
day lives we can choose to give significance to those
voices that are communicating the messages we want
to receive.

This truth has much relevance to our spiritual lives
as well. As we have already seen, we have an enemy
who is devoted to our destruction. Lives that are mired
in sin are also often filled with the lies and accusations of the Enemy. Our inner conversation becomes
a series of doubts, condemnations, and discouraging
thoughts. When we experience the grace of God, we
not only gain adoption as children of God, and become
heirs to the kingdom, we also receive God's sanctifying grace. Then, in addition to bearing witness with
our spirits that we are children of God, the Holy Spirit
also begins the ongoing work of telling us who we are
in Jesus. If we choose to allow that voice to become the
most significant voice in our lives, we can't help but
begin to become like who He says that we are.

Our salvation, of course, is based on faith alone.
Even that faith is a gift of God (see Ephesians 2:8–9).
But when the Bible speaks of faith, it is talking about
something more than simple assent to a proposition.
Faith is the kind of heartfelt belief that is willing to
stake its life on what it believes. It is the sort of belief
that comes not from hearing about faith or about
Jesus, but from an authentic life-changing encounter
with Jesus. And that faith is as important in cooper-
ating with sanctifying grace as it is in bringing us to

salvation in the first place. When we truly believe that Jesus is the way, the truth, and the life (see John 14:6), we are ready to fix our eyes upon Him, to open ourselves up to His grace, and to cooperate with Him as He give us the abundant life.

My Story

I was born into a churchgoing family who took the things of God seriously. My entire family was active in church throughout my childhood and adolescence. Our family home was a place of love and care for all. My parents provided for my needs and tried to instill in me appropriate reverence for God and good values in general. Despite these childhood blessings, as I have already shared, my adolescent years were marked by contradictions.

Though I attended church, and felt at home there, I was also a bit of a chameleon. In the summer between my elementary school years and the beginning of junior high school, our family made a move from a college town in Kentucky to coastal South Florida. I had a wonderful Kentucky childhood filled with good friends, a huge and loving extended family, and a strong sense of place. None of those things carried over to Florida. I was small for my age, a late bloomer, non-athletic, and awkward as a seventh grader. I spoke with a thick Kentucky accent in a school largely comprised of students who had moved from New York and New Jersey. Every time I opened my mouth, someone would laugh at how I said things. I was not immediately successful at making friends. And I deeply missed the Kentucky childhood I had left behind. After a couple of years of essentially a miserable junior high experience (I would later learn that it was not all that dissimilar to most people's junior high experience), I learned that my neighborhood was zoned for a high school that included almost no one from the junior high I attended. In essence, I would be starting over yet again in ninth grade.

I can still remember sitting on the beach during the summer before high school and deciding that some things needed to change. I was unhappy and the way I had been living didn't seem like it was working for me. I decided that I was going to be popular and powerful in high school and that I would do whatever I needed to do in order to accomplish those things. I essentially decided to become all things to all people. I hit high school with a vengeance.

When I was with the musicians, I tried to be a musician. I played in the marching band, the concert band, and the orchestra. If I was with the jocks, I tried (mostly unsuccessfully) to be a jock. I was on the wrestling team throughout high school, and even captained the team in my senior year. When I was at church, I played the pious believer. I managed to land several after-school jobs, and when I was at work, I played the role of a working guy. With the serious students, I tried to be studious. And then there was the drug crowd. Following my pattern, I went all in with them as well. And although it was hard to try to balance all of those different faces, I made a pretty successful go of it in high school. Though I wasn't really sure anymore who or what I really was, in my senior year I was band captain, wrestling team captain, editor of the school newspaper, a class officer, and a member of the National Honor Society. I had friends, in a manner of speaking, and I really thought that I was achieving my goals. The ultimate prize was when I received word that I was awarded a military scholarship to attend Vanderbilt University. In my mind, I revisited my plan and decided that it would just be more of the same at Vanderbilt.

During those adolescent years, I never really thought too deeply about God. I think I was sincere when I prayed and worshipped, but trying to be a good person and honoring God with my whole life just didn't seem to be delivering what I thought I needed from life.

Things began to seriously fall apart when I hit Vanderbilt. I had been what I thought of as a big fish in a fairly small pond in high school. Vanderbilt was a different story altogether. My family was of modest means, but I was now thrust into a world made up mostly of upper-class children of wealth. I can still remember the icebreaker from my freshman orientation small group. The leader kicked off the event by having everyone share about what they had done with their summer break. There were stories of grand tours of Europe, of cruises, of safaris, and other adventures. I shared with them that I had worked at a fast-food restaurant. I quickly discovered that I was now a very small fish in a much bigger lake, that no one cared what I had done in high school, and that my game plan was not going to work the way I had initially thought.

I did discover, however, a place where I could belong. It was a dive bar near the campus called the Speak Easy. This was not a student bar. It was a sawdust-floored hole-in-the-wall where locals went to drink too much. It had pinball and gambling machines, drug users in the darkened back corners, and lots of cheap draft beer. While I struggled to fit in other places, as long as I had money, I was the life of the party at the Speak Easy. I fit right in. And over the next couple of years my life began to spiral down, until my daily routine consisted of sleeping until around noon, trying to get a few things done until the bar opened at 3:00 in the afternoon, and then heading on over where I would stay until 3:00 a.m. closing or beyond. I would finally stagger home in the wee hours of the morning and try to sleep it off so that I could repeat the process the next day.

By the summer after my sophomore year, I was pretty close to the bottom. I was supposed to be taking summer school classes because I was way behind. But even that was a joke. I was failing out of school, constantly dirty, often broke, with a serious drinking problem, and I was in debt to a loan shark because I had started gambling to try to raise some quick funds to keep the party going. I also felt more alone than I had ever felt in my life when I discovered that my friends from the dive bar had all pretty much abandoned me when the money ran out.

I can still remember exactly what the summer school dorm room looked like the evening I decided that I needed to find a way out of the situation. I had very few personal items with me for summer school. Just a nearly empty desk, a small bed, a chair, and a few clothes. I was alone in the room and had pretty much decided that the only way out was to end my life. But, to be honest, I couldn't think of a way to do that without pain, and I was always kind of a wimp when it came to pain. So, I started trying to think of another solution. In my arrogance, I decided that what I really needed was a new plan. I took a pad of paper and reached in my desk drawer for a pen so that I could write out the plan. Instead of a pen, however, my hand closed around a small wooden cross.

I had not intentionally put that cross in the desk drawer, although I knew where it had come from. Someone from my home church had made them and given them to a group of youth who were on a choir tour that I had been part of. I had thrown it in a drawer back in Florida, and apparently it had wound up mixed with my pens and pencils.

As I stared at that wooden cross in my hand, a whirlwind of thoughts began racing through my mind. I thought about all the things I had heard about Jesus, and the cross, and how Jesus loved me, and had a plan for my life. And how if I would give Him my life, He would give me His. Honestly, not a lot of it made sense to me that evening. What did make sense was that I needed help and I had no other plan. So, alone in that dorm room, I cried out to Jesus. It didn't start off in the best way. I pretty much shouted at the Lord: "Okay, I don't have time to play around here. If You are real, and this is real, and You want my life, You can have it! But You need to do whatever You are going to do now! Change me, or whatever. Just do it!"

I was not a deeply religious person at the time, but did have enough sense to realize that if God really was listening, I might want to tone things down a bit. Eventually, I got on my knees and started pouring my heart out to God. I wasn't sure what I was supposed to do, but through my tears I confessed as best I knew how, and asked the Lord to forgive me. Then I said, "Lord, please don't ask me to be good. I don't even know if I know what that means. So, let's just do this.

I will give You my life, but You will have to show me what You want me to do. If You can make that clear to me, so that I can understand what You are asking me to do, I will do whatever that is. Can we just work it like that?"

I don't know if that is the right way to begin a relationship with Jesus or not. I was flying solo that night and that's just how Jesus and I did it. I fell asleep clutching that cross. It seemed to be my only hope.

When I awoke the next day, I still had every problem I had the evening before. I was still failing out of school. I was still dealing with addiction issues. I was still in serious debt and beyond broke. I didn't know how I was going to deal with any of that. But one thing I did know was that I was not alone. I knew, I mean I seriously *knew*, that Jesus was with me. If you have never experienced it before, I can't explain to you; and if you have experienced it, I don't need to. But I knew that, together, Jesus and I would be able to deal with what I was unable to do on my own. I experienced firsthand the grace of God. The Holy Spirit was bearing witness with my spirit that I was, indeed, a child of God and the Lord was alive within me. And right from that first moment, God began His sanctifying work within me.

The stories of all the adventures I have had with the Lord over the ensuing forty years would fill another book. Probably one that I need to write to give testimony to how amazing our Lord truly is. But during all those years, Jesus and I have operated with pretty much that same arrangement from the first night. I try to fix my gaze upon Him. I try to discern what He is telling me I should do, and I try to obey. I don't always get it right. Sometimes it is two steps forward and three steps back. But the Lord is always faithful, always present, always working, and always gracious. And little by little, He is transforming me.

Now, some who know me will say, "Wait a minute. I know you, and you aren't all that good!" One person told me some years ago, "I know people who aren't even believers who are better than you." And to be honest, I do too. There are a lot of really good people in the world. I'm blessed to know many. But here's the thing: If they are so good and they don't know Jesus, can you imagine how amazing they could be if they did? And if I'm so rotten, and I know Jesus, can you imagine how bad I would be if I didn't? Trust me, I can imagine. And no one wants to know that guy.

A lot of people believe that Jesus came to make good people out of bad people. And many people think that trying to be good is what Christianity is all about. But Jesus didn't come to make good people out of bad people. He came to make live people out of dead people. And through the power of His grace, He does just that. He's actually quite good at it. And when He says, "I have come that you might have life, and have it abundantly" (see John 10:10), He absolutely means that. My life was a complete wreck when Jesus came to me. Like that woman caught in adultery, I was guilty and stained with sin and caught dead to rights. And the voices of condemnation were surrounding me and growing. But Jesus said, "I don't condemn you. Let's go." I surrendered the mess that was my life, essentially worthless, and He gave me the kingdom in return. Amazing grace, indeed!

The Royal Purple of France

The story is told that back in the days when the kings ruled France with unquestioned authority, the royal tutors had some challenges in disciplining one young, headstrong crown prince. Apparently, the princeling, though still a child, was unruly, disrespectful, and generally impossible to deal with. The tutors were deeply frustrated by their charge and their inability to correct his erratic behavior.

The tutors' problem was further complicated by the rules for engagement with the young prince. As heir to the throne, he was not allowed to be touched by the tutors. Corporal punishment was out of the question. And even raising of the voice in anger was forbidden. Very little seemed to be effective in changing his behavior.

Then one day, the head tutor had an idea. He took a bolt of purple velvet, made in the color known as the royal purple of France. It was a color and fabric reserved only for the royal family. Cutting a small strip of the fabric, he pinned it on the prince's tunic, right over his heart. Then placing a hand gently over the boy's heart, he said, "Young man, this is the royal purple of France. It is your birthright. It represents everything your ancestors and forefathers bled and died for. It is the emblem of who you are. As you wear it, remember that everything you say and do is a reflection on that emblem. You must remember who you are and what you represent."

It is said that the young prince's behavior changed for the better almost immediately.

In a very real sense, those of us who have been touched and redeemed by the grace of Jesus Christ, made possible by His atoning sacrifice at the cross, are children of the King. We are royal princes and princesses in the kingdom of God. And although we have a heavenly Father who is good, and just, and whose mercies are new every morning (see Lamentations 3:22–23), we must also keep in mind that we bear the mark of the cross upon our breasts. It is everything our Lord bled and died for. It is the emblem of who we are. Our adoption into the royal family is the precious gift of God. In receiving it, however, we must remember that everything we say and do is a reflection on our Lord. We must never forget Whose we are, and what we represent.

SEVEN

Look Around

Then I heard the voice of the Lord saying, "Whom shall I send? And who will go for us?" And I said, "Here am I. Send me!"

—Isaiah 6:8

"But wait, there's more!" The breathless announcers peddling all manner of miracle products on late-night television invariably throw this phrase into their appeals. Having just extolled the virtues of the latest amazing vegetable slicer or snuggly throw pillow, they now have the incredible news that this wonderful deal is about to get better. There's more!

Of course, most of these television deals are not all that special, the products less than advertised. But the prospect of learning the whole story, of not missing out on any benefits of the deal, are often enough to keep us listening.

Isaiah's incredible encounter with the Lord has its own "but wait, there's more" moment. And this one is far more powerful, and significantly more important, than the chance to get a second Whopper Chopper for one low price. Isaiah has seen the Lord in all His glory. He has been personally broken before the Lord, only to experience the richness of God's grace in Jesus Christ. He is already tasting the abundant new life that begins the moment we embrace that grace. For many, all of these experiences would have been enough. But Isaiah discovered there was one more step in this adventure. And a vitally important step it is.

As Isaiah reports the scene, it is a relatively solitary affair. The Lord is present, seated on the throne in all His glory. The seraphim are there, praising the Lord and making their statement about His glory. And there is Isaiah, overwhelmed and overjoyed by his grace encounter. He is likely still experiencing the spiritual afterglow of his personal transformation. Yet, even in that ecstatic moment, Isaiah hears the Lord asking this question: "Whom shall I send?"

The question itself begs several additional questions: Send where? Send to do what? Send to whom? Send for how long? And all of these questions will be important down the line. But Isaiah immediately focuses on the "whom" in the Lord's question. And in doing so, he realizes that the answer is obvious.

I've often imagined this scene in my mind and chuckled a bit at God's sense of humor. Isaiah is standing there while the Lord is looking around as if trying to decide, when it dawns on Isaiah that he is really the only one there! God's question is rhetorical. Of course, Isaiah is the one the Lord seeks. God is calling Isaiah to join Him in His mission to the world, not because Isaiah is somehow special, but precisely because this is the response God seeks from every person who encounters and accepts the offer of God's grace in Jesus Christ.

Isaiah's response is immediate and unreserved, "Here am I. Send me!" I always imagine the Lord smiling in this moment. Isaiah gets it. He understands. And in agreeing to join the Lord in His mission in the world, he is also beginning a journey into everything he was created for. He is ready to truly experience the abundant life Jesus promised all of His followers.

Many followers of Jesus Christ in recent years have missed this part of the story. Even those who have been blessed with the experience of God's grace and who have trusted Jesus as their Savior and invited Him to be the Lord of their lives have often been content to let personal salvation be the end of the story. In these cases, Jesus becomes a get-out-of-jail-free card; His grace is nothing more than a spiritual fire insurance policy. God knows there is so much more.

We Are All Called!

"Do you think I am called to be a missionary?" I get the question all the time. As the president and CEO of a global mission agency, I guess it is natural that people would ask me this question. My response, however, is always a question a well: "Are you a Christ-follower?" If you are not a Christ-follower, you are most assuredly not called to be a missionary. But if you are a Christ-follower, there really is no question. Every follower of the Lord is called to join Jesus in His mission. As we stand before the throne, having tasted His grace, each of us should hear the Lord asking the same question Isaiah heard: "Whom shall I send?" And the expected reply is the same for us as it was for Isaiah. God is calling us, and God is counting on us.

So, if you are a Christ-follower, I have another question for you. (If you are not a Christ-follower, I'm still very pleased that you are reading this book. Please keep reading. But you are off the hook for this question.) What is it in your life that it takes Jesus Christ to explain? By that I mean, what are you doing in your life today, right now, that you wouldn't be doing were it not for Jesus Christ? What are you not doing that, apart from Jesus Christ, you surely would be doing? It what tangible ways is Jesus affecting or directing your life?

I came to this question many years ago in a somewhat surreal encounter in the middle of the night. During a season when I was planting a church in South Florida, I was also volunteering with Covenant House Ministries in Ft. Lauderdale, Florida. I was a part of their "Off the Streets" program at the time. In the evenings I would go out with a diminutive Roman Catholic nun (we made quite the pair on the streets) from around 10:00 in the evenings until around 2:00 or 3:00 in the morning searching for runaway and at-risk youth. Searching under bridges, behind dumpsters, on rooftops, and in the parks, we were trying to beat the predators of the night to these young people and get them to safety.

One evening at around 2:00 a.m. the nun said to me, "I need to check in with someone at a safe house for battered women. I want to stop there before we go back to Covenant House."

"That's fine," I replied, thinking nothing of her statement.

"Well, you need to understand. As a male, you are not allowed to know the exact location of the safe house. I'm going to need you to stay out at the van while I go in the complex to meet with this lady."

We proceeded to pull onto one of the toughest streets in Ft. Lauderdale. This was during the height of the crack cocaine epidemic in South Florida. The block-long street was dark and menacing, and there were crack dealers located on both street corners. The nun disappeared into an apartment complex in the middle of the block, and I was left standing beside our panel van on the side of the road. As I leaned against the van, with my Covenant House ID badge gleaming in the streetlights, I watched the scene playing out on the street corners. A car would approach the crack dealers on one corner, slow to a crawl, roll down the window, and then see me. Apparently assuming I must be a police officer, they would suddenly step on the gas and screech away. And the crack dealers would look angrily down the street in my direction. Then a few moments later, the same scene would play out on the other street corner. After three or four similar occurrences, I looked up to see one of the largest men I had ever seen in my life heading toward me. As he approached, I noted that his teeth were clenched, his jaw was set, and there was anger in his eyes. And because I have the gift of discernment, I said to myself: *You know he's not happy!*

Actually, what I really did in that moment was look up and say to the Lord, "You know that place You went to prepare for me? Call room service, because I'll be checking in there really soon." I just couldn't imagine any way this encounter was going to end well. About that time, the crack dealer was in front of me.

"Who are you, and what are you doing here?" he demanded angrily.

"I'm Max and I'm with Covenant House," I said softly.

"Covenant House? Y'all the ones who do things for the little kids?"

"Yes, that's us," I said.

"Well, why do you do this anyway?" he asked.

I thought to myself: *You know, that's a good question. I was just asking myself the same thing!* Have you ever had a situation where you surprised yourself with what you said or where you opened your mouth without knowing exactly what was about to come out? It was like that for me on this night. I heard myself saying to this man: "I don't know. I'm just a guy who loves Jesus and right now I think this is where Jesus wants me to be."

"Oh, so you're religious?" he asked with a hint of sarcasm.

"Man, I don't know if I'm religious or not," I said. "I'm just a guy who loves Jesus and right now I think this is where He wants me to be."

The man looked at me hard for a moment and then one single tear began to trickle down his right cheek, glistening in the streetlight. He softened his tone a bit and said to me, "You know, you probably think I'm a bad man . . . and maybe I am. But you're alright. And the stuff you are doing for the kids, that's alright too. Don't you worry about anything. You just keep doing what you are doing."

He paused for a moment and then said, "Who knows, maybe I'll do something good for people someday too." Then he turned and walked away into the night.

Now, I'm a pastor. I want to tell you that the man fell on his face on the sidewalk, gave his life to Jesus, and today he's a megachurch pastor or something. That would be a great story. But it didn't happen that way. I don't know where that man ended up. He may be in jail or he may be the governor of Florida, for all I know. But this much I do know: as I was driving home at 3:00 that morning, something occurred to me. If I'm a Christ-follower, why are there not more moments like that in my life? I'm not talking about encounters with crack dealers in the middle of the night. I don't recommend that. I mean, why are there not more moments when the only explanation is Jesus?

If Jesus is my Lord, if I'm truly following Him, shouldn't there regularly, even daily, be moments when the only answer to the question "Why do you do this anyway?" is Jesus. And shouldn't Jesus be the explanation for more and more of my life as I grow in my capacity to follow Him? So, I return to the question for Christ-followers: What is it in your life that it takes Jesus Christ to explain?

On Mission with God

On that evening in Ft. Lauderdale, I was on mission. Having said to the Lord, "Here am I. Send me!" the Lord had answered by sending me to the streets. Sending on mission is what Jesus does. Always. And joining Jesus in His mission is the primary calling of every Christ-follower.

I don't usually use the term *missions* with an "s." The truth is that there are multitudes of missions in the world, and pretty much everyone is on one mission or another. For some, the mission is trying to beat a little white ball around in a pasture until they can force it into a hole in the ground. For others, it is to binge-watch every episode of some television sitcom on Netflix, or to get the highest score on whatever the latest game craze is on iPhone. The possibilities are endless. But for all the possibilities, there is truly only one mission that has eternal consequences and eternal significance. That is, of course, the mission of Jesus. And it is to that specific mission that all Christ-followers are called.

Indeed, mission is the reason the church exists. The church (or the set apart, called out people of God, which is the original meaning of the word *church*) began at Pentecost. Prior to that amazing day, there was no church. When the Holy Spirit appeared like a rushing wind, and tongues of fire propelled the previously frightened and secluded apostles into the streets to proclaim the good news of the kingdom of God with boldness, the church was born. And if the church began at Pentecost, the stage was set for Pentecost a few weeks earlier at the Mount of Olives when Jesus held His last meeting with His followers before ascending into heaven.

According to Luke, who gives us the account of this incredible moment in the first chapter of the book of Acts, all of the disciples were gathered around Jesus as He prepared to leave them. They had been with Him through three years of teaching and ministry, through the events leading up to the crucifixion, and through the strange and exciting days following His resurrection as they came to terms with their new reality and His continued presence with them. Now, however, the moment they had dreaded was upon them; He was leaving. And the most important ques-tion on their minds in that moment, according to Luke, was "When are You coming back?" "When will

You restore the kingdom?" they wanted to know. "Tell us about how this all ends." "When are You coming back?" It is totally understandable that this would be of interest to the disciples. What is surprising is Jesus' answer: "That's none of your stinking business!"

Okay, perhaps that is my paraphrase of what Jesus said. According to Luke, "He said to them: 'It is not for you to know the times or the dates the Father has set by his own authority'" (Acts 1:7). Although Jesus' words are much more artful and gracious, they still pretty much mean, "It's none of your stinking business." Jesus says we should not be worried about when He is coming back. That is something between Him and the Father. For us, it is a matter of faith and trust, and is best left up to God. Instead, Jesus tells the disciples to get down to Jerusalem, get in a prayer meeting, and wait for the promised Holy Spirit. And then He tells them why: "You will receive power when the Holy Spirit comes on you; and you will be my witnesses in Jerusalem, and in all Judea and Samaria, and to the ends of the earth" (v. 8).

When Jesus had spoken these words, He ascended into the clouds and disappeared. The disciples, however, stood and stared openmouthed into the heavens. And to be honest, I'm quite sure I would have been doing the same. It isn't every day that you see someone ascend into the heavens and disappear, especially when that someone is Jesus! I love what happens next: a couple of angels appear from the depths of the clouds and get the attention of the disciples.

"Hey, why are you standing around staring into the heavens! Didn't Jesus just give you something to do?" And, of course, that something—get down to Jerusalem, get in a prayer meeting, get filled with the Holy Spirit and power—was all for the sake of the church. The church was launched in that prayer/Holy Spirit power meeting. And we must not miss this truth: the power Jesus spoke about was directly connected to the mission! Again, mission is the reason the church exists!

In some circles I've had people challenge me by saying, "Well, surely worship is the reason the church exists!" While there is no question that worship is important, and a vital part of healthy church life, worship was already going on before the church ever existed. Not only was worship regular and central to the everyday lives of the early disciples, in both the temple and the synagogue, according to Luke they continued to worship in the temple every day even after Pentecost (see Acts 2:46). God did not have a worship problem before the church. He did, however, have a mission problem. The church is God's answer to that problem. Yet, the church of today is often not on mission.

In the next chapter we will look more deeply into why mission is the reason the church exists, and what that means for our lives and calling. For now, let's look at why many followers of Jesus are not joining Him in His mission. What are they doing instead? What is distracting Christ-followers from the mission?

To answer this question, we must again bear in mind that we have an enemy. He is a liar, a deceiver, and he is totally opposed to the mission of Jesus. You may choose to call him the Devil, or Satan, or the Enemy, or the Accuser, or simply the presence of evil in the world. This enemy confronted Jesus (unsuccessfully) and he is still confronting God's church today. Distraction is one of his most effective tools.

The Three Distractions of the Deceiver

Satan may be many things, but creative is not one of those things. The Lord creates. Satan only perverts and distorts that which has been created. It has always been this way. And because Satan is not creative, it is relatively simple to discern his deceptions and the tools of his trade. When he tried, unsuccessfully, to tempt Jesus, he gave us access to his plan of action. We can assume that Satan brought his best efforts in trying to test Jesus; therefore, looking at those three temptations helps us understand what we can expect from our deceptive enemy.

The temptations of Jesus can really be boiled down to three basic concepts. Satan tried to tempt Jesus to take shortcuts to feel good, to look good, and to have goods. That's it. Rather than pursuing the purpose for which He was created, the tempter tried to divert Jesus to pursue pleasure for its own sake, or prestige and power for their own sake, or possessions and wealth as an endgame. Jesus understood the lie behind all of these temptations. He knew that the Enemy is a liar, and that the promises made in pursuing these things as ends in and of themselves are always false and fleeting. Further, Jesus knew that His Father desired to give Him all of these things as by-products of living a faithful life and pursuing His life's purpose. Satan failed, of course, in his attempts to sidetrack Jesus. Sadly, although he is still using the same old tired temptations with the rest of us, he is far more successful with many today than he was with Jesus. Let's look at how this plays out.

The Pleasure Temptation

Although the Declaration of Independence of the United States of America lists the pursuit of happiness as an unalienable right, that doesn't make it something worth pursuing. Indeed, the idea that pursuing happiness is a worthy life goal constitutes one of the strongest lies of the Enemy, and it is a lie that has grown ever stronger in contemporary society.

Most people these days give very little thought to the meaning of life. If you stop random people on the streets of the United States and ask them what they believe to be the meaning of life, most will answer with a blank stare. When people do answer with anything, the response is often something such as: "I guess it is just to try to be happy." There is nothing inherently wrong with happiness. Being happy can be a good thing, and most people welcome happiness in their lives. The problem is that no healthy person is happy all the time. The word *happy* derives from the word *happenstance* precisely because happiness is not all that predictable. It is usually the result of happenstance. Sometimes we are happy and sometimes we are not.

Additionally, while happiness is a wonderful by-product of pursuing other worthwhile things, it doesn't work well when we pursue it as an end unto itself. Further, in our society when we try to pursue happiness, it usually means pursuing pleasure. And so much of what the Enemy tempts us with concerns shortcuts in the pursuit of pleasure.

The problem lies in the very nature of pleasure pursuits. In every case, pursuing pleasure as the aim of life fails precisely because, in pursuing pleasure, it always takes more and more to produce less and less. Ultimately, this reality creates a life that is giving everything and gaining nothing at all.

Take drug and alcohol addiction, for instance. Any honest addict, or at least an addict who is trying to get honest, will admit that every subsequent high is nothing but a vain attempt to reproduce the first high. Let's be honest, people abuse drugs and alcohol because they bring pleasure—at first. No one would continue to abuse them if this weren't so. The lie comes into play when people learn that in addiction it always takes more and more to produce less and less until the day comes when they are giving their whole life and getting nothing in return. And the Enemy laughs.

The same is true with illicit sexual encounters. So many lives have been ruined by the promise of a pleasurable liaison that resulted in a few fleeting moments of pleasure and a lifetime of pain and broken relationships. The growing struggles with gluttony, conspicuous consumption, and adventure-chasing behavior in our society today are all signs that this temptation to pursue pleasure for its own ends is gaining traction. And the results are always, sadly, the same.

Having fasted for forty days, Jesus must have been famished. At that point, I'm sure there was nothing that seemed more pleasurable than food. He understood, however, that to compromise His mission for the fleeting happiness of some illicitly gotten bread, though momentarily pleasurable, would not have delivered long-term happiness, nor the joy that was set before Him in His mission. He was not willing to take shortcuts to feel good.

Pleasure is a wonderful by-product of other worthy pursuits. And the Lord wants us to know the gift of His pleasure. If the Enemy is able to sidetrack us from that for which we were created by false promises of the results of pursuing pleasure, he knows that we will, in the end, receive neither the pleasure he promised nor the abundant life we could have had in Jesus Christ.

The Prestige Temptation

Many years ago, a Hollywood celebrity known for his sartorial elegance and his handsome, youthful appearance, repeatedly assured the world that, "It is better to look good than to feel good." In any era, this is an absurd proposition. Sadly, however, the sentiments expressed by this vacuous actor hit all too close to home in today's shallow world. The idea that it is better to look good than to feel good represents another lie of the Enemy. If Satan can't get us to give our lives away trying to feel good, he will often tempt us to something even more vapid: the temptation to pursue looking good.

It has often been said that reputation is what a person is in the daylight and character is what that same person is in the dark of night. But much of current culture is more concerned with reputation than character. We pursue personal power, prestige, or position as if life will flow from these things. We believe we will find meaning in the number of people reporting to us at work, or the number of followers we have on social media, or the number of exclusive clubs to which we have access. And even as we pursue these things, we turn a blind eye to the mounting evidence that these pursuits never produce a meaningful life.

Not only is fame fleeting, it is also lonely and life-less. Witness the growing number of celebrities at the top of their game who take their own lives, or live a sham life as a result of debilitating addictions and dangerous pursuits. We see the old adage that power tends to corrupt being played out in the halls of power all over the world on a daily basis. And many people who have clawed their way to the top of the positional ladder only discover too late just how lonely and isolated life can be at the top.

Satan tried this temptation with Jesus as well: "Throw yourself off the pinnacle of the temple," he said. "Angels will come and rescue you!" (see Luke 4:9–11). The implication was clear: You will show Your power in a dramatic way. You'll let everyone see who is really in charge. You'll be famous. Of course, this tempta-tion failed with Jesus. But many of His followers have nevertheless given in to its subtle pull.

Again, none of these things are inherently prob-lematic. As the outcome of a life of purpose and meaning they can each be quite worthwhile. A good reputation, and even a measure of fame, built through a life of devotion to meaningful pursuits is often desir-able. The sacrifices of leadership can be worth the cost when someone is called on by others to give leadership to worthy endeavors. And Jesus Himself promised His followers power, though not power for its own sake. The power was not for the sake of making those who were empowered to look good, but for the sake of the mission. Thus, it is not position, power, or prestige that are problematic, but the temptation to pursue these things as ends in and of themselves in order to make ourselves look good.

The Possessions Temptation

Perhaps the most insidious of the three temptations of the Enemy concerns our possessions: the temptation to have goods. Although equally as empty as the first two, this temptation is the very basis of our consumer-driven world. The idea is largely captured by a bumper sticker I saw a while back: "The one who dies with the most toys . . . wins!"

Isn't that the craziest idea you have ever heard? Here's a news flash: the one who dies with the most toys . . . is dead! And we aren't taking any of our possessions with us. I've done many funerals over the years, and have never seen a hearse pulling a U-Haul. It all gets left behind. Yet we continue to pile up more and more stuff, as if somehow we are one more purchase away from meaning and fulfillment.

Howard Hughes, at the time one of the wealthiest (and unhappiest) people on the planet, was asked: "How much is enough?" He quickly replied: "Just a little bit more." Here lies the real heart of the lie of this temptation to acquire possessions. There is never enough. There are always larger houses, more expensive cars, fancier and more costly clothes. And, in the end, all of these possessions end up controlling us. We live and work just to pay for and keep up with our stuff. One of the fastest-growing and most lucrative industries in the United States is the storage unit rental business. We have filled our lives with so much stuff that we have to buy a place outside of our homes to store the excess so that we have room for all the new stuff we have to have.

Satan tried to tempt Jesus with literally everything. If Jesus would simply bow down and worship

him, Satan promised to give it all to Jesus. All the kingdoms and wealth of the world. All the stuff! Jesus, of
course, was not willing to sell His soul for possessions,
no matter how great the offer. Our consumer society
has largely decided that Jesus made the wrong choice.

As with pleasure and prestige, there is nothing
wrong with possessions. The Lord makes it clear that
He knows our needs for food, shelter, clothing, and
security. Recall His promise in Matthew 6:33 that if
we will seek first the kingdom of God and God's righteousness, all these other things will be given to us as
well. As with the other two temptations, the problem
is not the possessions themselves, but the pursuit of
possessions as the aim of our lives, rather than seeking
first the purposes of God.

It is no wonder that many Christ-followers are not
engaged in the mission of Jesus in any meaningful
way. Our lives are often so distracted in pursuing pleasure, prestige, and possessions that there is no time
left over to even consider the mission. Fortunately,
there is good news. God not only has a plan, He also
has things to offer for those who will join Jesus in His
mission. And unlike the false claims of the Enemy,
God's promises deliver!

God's Alternative: The Promises of Mission

When Isaiah, in the clear light of God's glory, looked
around and saw the world as the Lord was seeing it,
he saw the need and the brokenness. And when the
Lord asked that vitally important question, "Whom
shall I send?" Isaiah understood that if he answered
the call, he would not be sent alone and unprepared. In
agreeing to be sent, Isaiah understood that he was not

embarking on an assignment to engage the world for God. Instead, he was heading into a journey with God and into the work of God in the world, a work that was already ongoing even as Isaiah joined in. And a work that is still ongoing.

One of my dear friends tells the story of getting on an airplane in Atlanta that was headed for Costa Rica. Joining him on that trip was a group of excited and enthusiastic young people from a church in the United States. They were headed to Costa Rica on a short-term mission trip. My friend didn't have to ask the purpose of their trip, because each member of the team was adorned in a glowing yellow shirt emblazoned with the words: "Taking Jesus to Costa Rica!"

Although these young people undoubtedly had good hearts and intentions, the shirts were just wrong on so many levels. A whole book could be written about some of the missiological problems with the statement made by their shirts. At the top of the list would be the assumption that the bright young men and women were taking Jesus somewhere. Jesus is already present and working in Costa Rica, and He has been forever. In addition, we don't go on mission for Jesus, we go with Him. And we don't go to build something for the Lord. We go to seek and discover what the Lord is already doing and join Him in that. The mission is His mission. We are sent with Him! As we go, we can be sure that He equips us for the mission and for life.

There Is Power When We Are on Mission

As we've already seen, Jesus promised that the church would receive power when the Holy Spirit came, and He connected that power to the mission. The church would be empowered in order that it might witness for Him. Both at home and around the world. While the Enemy tempts us to try to acquire power for its own sake, Jesus promises us that we will be empowered by the Holy Spirit as we join Him in His mission. There is power when we are on mission.

I came to understand more about this missional power during a trip to India many years ago. I'm not the smartest little bunny who ever hopped out of a hutch, and I proved that yet again by scheduling my trip during the Indian monsoon. It rains during monsoon. A lot. All the time. Indeed, thirty-seven inches of rain fell in one day in Mumbai during the monsoon, creating raging rivers out of the streets and killing thousands. This is serious rain. So, I went to India during this season. And I met Raj.

Raj was a member of one of the lowest rungs on the Hindu caste system. He was poor, lacked formal education, and was not highly respected by his own people. But Raj loved Jesus, owned a Bible, and had devoted himself to going into Dalit villages to tell the people about Jesus. (Dalits are sometimes referred to as "untouchables" or "unscheduled caste" and are at the bottom of the Hindu system.) When I met Raj, he was excited to tell me about a village where he had been preaching for the past eight weeks. He told me that the following Sunday he would be giving a message and inviting the people in the village for the first time to trust in Jesus. He asked if I would like to go with him. "There is no place I'd rather be," I replied.

On Sunday morning, our driver, who was Muslim, picked us up to head out for the village. As we drove, the driver said, "Raj, you know the people of the village all think that your God is a powerful God."

"Well, my God is a powerful God," Raj replied. "But why are they saying this?"

"Don't you realize," the driver replied, "you have been speaking in this village for eight weeks and it is monsoon, yet it has never rained while you were there."

"This might not be good," Raj said softly, beginning to worry about the weather. This Dalit village had no church building, of course, nor any other indoor space for the gathering. The speaking was taking place in an outdoor muddy patch in the community.

We arrived and got set up, and again it was not raining. That situation changed quickly, however, nearly as soon as Raj began to speak. Thick dark clouds came racing across the sky and rain began to fall harder than I had ever experienced in my life. We could see the water rising on the ground as trash and excrement began to float on the water. I started looking around for somewhere to flee from the rain, as did all of the villagers. But not Raj. I noticed that he was looking at the clouds and muttering to himself. Then suddenly, he pointed at the clouds and said in a commanding voice: "No! This is not monsoon. This is Satan! In the name of Jesus Christ, stop this rain!"

I'm sorry to admit that I was trying to get Raj's attention to signal to him that this was a bad idea. I was thinking: *We don't do weather!* But Raj was already in action. And I think the villagers and I were equally surprised when, in response to Raj's rebuke, the downpour slowed to just a drizzle. I stopped and looked, my eyes wide with amazement. The villagers stopped to watch, also wide-eyed. I was so impressed, I thought we should take an offering! But not Raj. He wasn't at all satisfied. He dropped to his knees in that filthy water, spread his arms wide, and shouted out: "No! You are not a God who does things halfway. In the name of Jesus Christ . . . Stop . . . This. . . Rain!"

And, immediately, the rain stopped. I mean *completely* stopped. In fact, a little hole opened up in the clouds and some rays of sunshine shone into the village. I don't guess I need to tell you that villagers were falling all over themselves that day to trust and follow Jesus. It was a remarkable day.

As we were leaving the village, I said, "You know, Raj, you are powerful man. I just don't normally see things like that."

Raj looked at me as if I were a crazy man. He said, "Powerful man? I'm poor, uneducated, and I don't even have the respect of my own people. I have no power. None at all. Now, my God . . . my God is a powerful God." Then he looked at me seriously and said, "Do you know why you don't see things like this?"

"Tell me," I replied.

"It's because you don't preach the gospel."

Now, I know I am not the greatest preacher who ever lived, but I had, at that time, been preaching for more than two decades. I looked at Raj and said softly, "You know, I do think I preach the gospel."

"I know you do," he said, "and that's the problem."

"Help me understand what you are saying," I replied uncertainly.

"Well, what is the gospel?"

"It is the good news of Jesus Christ," I replied.

"I agree," Raj said. "So, let me ask you: Is it always good?"

I wasn't sure where he was going with this, but I thought about it for a minute and then said, "Yes, Raj, I believe it is always good."

"I do too," he said. "But here's another question: Is it always news?"

Suddenly, I began to see where he was going. "No, I suppose it isn't always news," I said.

"And here is the problem. In the United States, you guys like to gather up the already-convinced each week inside a building. Then you bring the pastor out on stage where he or she goes over the story once again, as everyone sits silently making sure the pastor still knows the story. And then everyone goes home and lives as if nothing that was said matters at all, until the following week, when they all gather again in the same place and bring the pastor back out to go over the story one more time."

Then he asked me: "Do you know what Romans 1:16 says?"

He caught me on a good day, because I did know: "I am not ashamed of the gospel of Christ, for it is the power of God . . ." (NKJV).

"Stop!" he said, when I got to "the power of God." "Do you see it? Do you see what this says? The gospel and the power of God are connected. You can't tear them apart. And if the gospel is the good news of Jesus Christ, then I can give you a promise: if you will get busy taking the good news to places where it is not only good, but also news, you will unleash the power of God!"

And he was right, of course. Jesus promised us power. Power for the mission. And He sent us to proclaim the good news of the kingdom throughout the world. But good news is only news if it hasn't already been heard over and over again.

We can be encouraged, however, by the fact that all of us are surrounded by people for whom it is news. For some, it may be news to someone who sleeps in a bedroom in your own home, or to a next-door neighbor. Perhaps it is news to someone at our place of work or to the cashier we speak to every day at our favorite coffee shop. For others, it might be people trapped in poverty or addiction or prison who have never heard. And, of course, there are more than two billion people on the planet living in places where no one has ever heard the good news of Jesus Christ.

There is power when we are on mission. And we can unleash that power when we get busy taking the good news to where it is not only good, but also news.

There Is Purpose When We Are on Mission

For those who believe that the whole point of the good news, the gospel message, is our personal salvation, did you ever wonder why God doesn't just call us home the moment we trust Jesus? I mean, seriously, if we have made a decision and experienced the grace of God, if like Isaiah, we've heard the pronouncement that we are clean, why not just have the Lord zap us and take us on to heaven before we have a chance to mess it all up again? We make a profession of faith, the lightning bolt comes, and we're standing in front of the pearly gates awaiting our admission.

Obviously, faith life doesn't work that way. And for good reason. When you really think about it, there are only two things we can do on earth that we can't do

in heaven. One is to continue in sin. In the fullness of
the presence of God and the light of His glory, even the
idea of sin will be a long-forgotten thing. There will
be no sin in heaven. The second is to join Jesus in His
mission in the world. Once we are in heaven, everyone
will know exactly who Jesus is and will be in His presence forever. His kingdom will be established for all
eternity and there will be no more need to share the
good news of the kingdom of God. Everything else we
could do just as well in heaven as we can on earth. If
the Lord leaves His disciples on earth once they have
accepted Him as Lord, it must be for one or the other
of these two purposes. And since He came to show us
the way to break the power of sin, I think it is clear He
didn't leave us here to continue in sin. Thus, we can
assume we were left here for the purpose of joining
Him in His mission.

In Paul's letter to the church at Ephesus, he gives a
wonderfully simple explanation of the gospel: "For it is
by grace that you have been saved, through faith—and
this is not from yourselves, it is the gift of God—not
by works, so that no one can boast" (Eph. 2:8–9). This
is the gospel in a nutshell. Grace, through faith, is the
gift of God. It's all there. But oftentimes we stop at the
end of verse 9. Paul didn't. He went on, saying: "For
we are God's handiwork, created in Christ Jesus to do
good works, which God prepared in advance for us to
do" (v. 10).

The "we" in Ephesians 2:10 is those of us who
have been saved by grace, through faith; in other
words, Christ-followers. Paul says at the new birth,
and through the sanctification process, we have been
"created in Christ Jesus"—re-created, really, and that,
with a purpose. And the purpose is clear: "to do good

works." But not just any good works will do. Paul says there are works that "God prepared in advance" just for us to do. Now, this is not some good works assignment so that we can earn our way to God's favor or to heaven. Paul has already ruled that out in verse 9. Instead, these good works that God prepared in advance for us are a part of that grace that saves us. These good works are a part of the abundant life that Jesus promised us. These works get at the core of our purpose. And I don't believe any of us will ever fully experience the abundant life that Jesus promised until we join Him in His mission in the way that He has specifically created us to do, and in doing the things He prepared in advance for us to do. There is something marvelous and wonderful about being around someone who has discovered that purpose and is living it out. There is truly life in these people, and it is abundant!

When I first met Fred, he was the Sunday school superintendent of a church I was serving in a small rural community in Florida. Fred was a retiree with a servant heart and a willingness to take on tasks that needed to be done. And each week I would watch as he went from classroom to classroom in the church on Sunday morning, carrying out his responsibilities. He was very faithful. But his slumping shoulders, somewhat melancholy expression, and the weariness in his voice suggested to me that Fred was not at all happy in this role. When I would ask Fred about this, he always dutifully replied, "Well, Pastor, it's okay. Someone has to do this job." But it just didn't suit Fred.

Some months into my tenure at Fred's church, we started trying to teach the idea that God had a design and purpose for each of Jesus' disciples. We developed (and liberally borrowed) some tools for helping people discover for themselves just what this design might be. I ended up being Fred's coach in the process. After several weeks of looking at a number of things, I asked Fred again: "Do you enjoy being Sunday school superintendent?" He started to give me his usual servant-hearted answer, but I stopped him. "Fred, you don't really like doing that very much, do you?" He looked down at the floor and said, "No, not really." I can't say I was surprised.

"Okay, Fred, here's what I want you to do: When we finish here, go home and get a box and put all of the superintendent things in it. Then bring them over to the church and leave them outside my office door."

Fred looked surprised: "Are you firing me, Pastor?"

"No, Fred, I'm not firing you. I'll get someone else to do that job. We're going to find something that works better for you. What do you think you would really like to do if nothing could stand in your way?"

Fred stared at the floor for a couple of minutes and then looked up and sheepishly said, "Well, if you want to know the truth, I've always wanted to be a clown!"

I have to admit, his answer shocked me on several levels. For one, I had a hard time envisioning our melancholy superintendent as a clown. And, to be honest, I've never really liked clowns. I just couldn't see where this was going at all. But Fred was on a roll.

"I was thinking that I could take clown lessons, and maybe get some other people interested in it too, and we could have a clown ministry, and maybe do things in the worship service . . ." As he spoke, he became more and more animated and excited. I had never seen Fred like this. And although the idea of having clowns in the worship service didn't appeal to me at all, I had to admit that as I looked at Fred's profile, it did seem that some kind of ministry in this area might be a fit for him. But I seriously doubted if Fred was going to find much interest in this conservative, rural town for his seemingly crazy idea.

"I'll tell you what, Fred, why don't you look into it? I mean, I don't even know who gives clown lessons. And I don't know if there would be any interest from others. And we'd need a ministry plan. But sure, you can check things out." I honestly didn't expect anything to come of it. I could not have been more wrong.

It turns out that there are professional clown trainers (who knew?) and given our proximity to Sarasota, Florida, home of the Ringling Brothers and Barnum and Bailey, our area actually had an abundance of them. It wasn't more than a few weeks later when Fred came to me to announce that nine people in the church were taking formal clown lessons and would be ready to go in a couple more months. "And then we can do something in the worship service!" Fred was very eager.

My heart sank a little. "Well, let's go slowly, Fred. Why don't we see if there are some things your clowns could do with the children's ministry and in some other areas?"

"And then we can do something in the worship services?" Fred asked.

"We'll see . . ." I replied, though my heart wasn't in it.

Two months later, I was invited to the graduation event for our new clowns. I was impressed. Each of the clowns had made his or her own costume, had learned to do very professional makeup jobs, and each clown had a unique name and personality. They had really put a lot of time and energy into it. And they were good.

Fred began having the clowns help out in our children's ministry area. The clowns also began to help with some of our community outreach ministries. And because our small town loved to have parades, the clowns began to regularly work those as well. In the holiday season, they would be on the parade routes, making people laugh and offering up candy and invitations to holiday worship experiences. They also began attracting more clowns!

One day Fred came to see me. "Pastor, we now have twenty-five trained clowns in the church!"

"Fred, what on earth are you going to do with all those clowns?" I asked.

"Oh, Pastor, with the nursing home ministries growing the way they are, we can hardly keep up!"

"What nursing home ministry?" I asked, perplexed.

"Oh, you haven't heard about that? Well, at one of the parades some time ago a woman approached me about coming to visit some of the people in the nursing home where she worked. She explained to me that studies have shown that their residents, especially some who have been noncommunicative for a while, will often open up to clowns. They don't know exactly why. Maybe it is the exaggerated facial features, or it reverts them back to childhood or something. But she said it would be a big help. So, we went.

"Well, it turns out she was right. And some of our clowns actually enjoyed this kind of ministry as well. We were really making a difference. But word got out, and another nursing home called, and, well . . . we are now working in nine different nursing homes! It is getting hard to keep up. We need more clowns!"

"Oh, and one more thing, Pastor," Fred said with a smile, "can we do something in the worship services now?"

"One time, Fred. One time," I replied. Though by now I knew it would be an ongoing thing. Those clowns were making an impact all over the community. They were touching lives, doing kingdom work, truly joining Jesus in His mission, albeit in an unusual way.

The best part of all, for me, was watching the transition in Fred. I used to ask him regularly if he wanted to continue being superintendent. I actually felt bad for him. But I never once asked Fred if he wanted to continue with the clowns. There was a spring in his step and a twinkle in his eyes. He had found his purpose. And for him this wasn't works, this was life! Abundant life. And neither he nor that community were ever the same as a result.

There is purpose when we are on mission! And a life lived on purpose is a big part of living the abundant life in Jesus.

There Is Provision When We Are on Mission

Sometimes I think Christ-followers have a bizarre idea of how God operates. It's as if we think God is out there somewhere in the clouds gathering the angels together like a cosmic prankster: "Hey, angels, look at this. You see that guy Max? This is going to be hilarious! I've convinced him that he is called to join Me in the mission, but I'm not going to give him anything he needs to succeed. He's going to fall flat on his face! Won't that be funny?"

Is that the kind of God you serve? Have you ever known God to act that way with any of His children? Of course not! Yet we sometimes act as if God is unwilling or unable to provide the things we need for the mission to which we've been called.

"I was young and now I am old, yet I have never seen the righteous forsaken or their children begging bread" (Ps. 37:25). The psalmist knows the truth. Our God is a God of provision and He loves to provide for the missional needs of those who join Him in the mission. The Bible says that God owns "the cattle on a thousand hills" (Ps. 50:10) and that He loves to "give good gifts" to His children (Matt. 7:11). When King David was consecrating the offering for the building of the temple, he prayed these beautiful words:

> Yours, Lord, is the greatness and the power
> > and the glory and the majesty and
> > > the splendor,
> > for everything in heaven and earth
> > > is yours.
> Yours, Lord, is the kingdom;
> > you are exalted as head over all.
> Wealth and honor come from you;
> > you are the ruler of all things.
> In your hands are strength and power
> > to exalt and give strength to all.
> > > (1 Chron. 29:11–12)

The Lord has the resources and gifts we need to carry out anything He calls us to do. And the Lord loves to share those gifts and resources. And although He is the source of all provision, He has chosen to scatter those resources among His people so that we can all participate in both the mission and the provision.

Back in the early 2000s, I was pastoring a church in Gainesville, Florida. It was (and is) a great church. At the time I became the pastor, the church was eleven years old. Together, this faith community was doing a lot quite well, and lives were being changed as a result. The church's mission outreach, however, had been compartmentalized. A group of about a dozen gifted and energetic men and women made an annual pilgrimage to Haiti on a short-term medical mission trip, and the church budgeted approximately twenty-three thousand dollars each year to be parceled out among a number of local and international ministries. They were on mission, but just barely. And the idea that mission is the reason the church exists was, for this church, a new way of thinking.

We brought in an outside consultant working with a mission-sending agency named The Mission Society (TMS Global, today) to help our church get a strategic plan for mission and also work out how that mission would be funded. As part of the model we adopted, we would hold an annual Global Impact Celebration, which culminated in a faith promise offering. This once-a-year offering commitment would fund our local and global outreach for the coming year.

Reverend Dick McClain, our coach for the first Global Impact Celebration, encouraged me to consider a financial goal for the faith promise offering. I was hesitant, having never done anything like this before and being brand-new at this church. But Dick insisted, and after some prayer, I said: "How about $75,000?" That was a little more than three times what we had been doing, and it seemed a reasonable, if somewhat ambitious, goal. We put it out there.

Now I had a problem, however. The idea behind faith promise is that each person seeks the Lord, asking how much they can trust the Lord to sow into their lives in the coming year, which they can then steward by faithfully giving it to the mission of the church. It is a commitment of trust and faith between the person making the commitment and God. Sometimes the funds to fulfill the commitment come from miraculous and surprising sources, other times from people's commitment to make life changes or seek additional revenues in their lives. It varies from person to person. I was prepared to ask the congregation to make this kind of commitment for the first time. I have never asked a congregation I have pastored to do something that I was unwilling to do myself, and I knew that meant my wife and I would have to make a faith promise ourselves. And I was happy to do so. The problem was deciding how much it should be.

We were encouraging people to ask God and trust the response they received. And I believed God would direct. But I wasn't hearing anything. My wife and I were already tithing our paychecks to the local church, we were sponsoring several children each month through Compassion International, and we were sending small monthly support checks to several missionaries. I just wasn't sure how much more we could do.

Now, I need to confess something. I have an addiction, and confessing it will probably require me to turn in my Southerner card. I am addicted to unsweetened iced tea! I drink it all day, every day. Lots of it. And in Gainesville, my go-to source for my unsweet tea was the Krystal fast-food restaurant. The tea was good, but what I really liked was the cup size. They served a size called a "Roadie" that was like a small trash can with a straw! They needed a winch to get it through the drive-through window into the car! And I was getting three or four of them a day, every day.

One particular day, I was fussing at Jesus about the faith promise thing. Sometimes Jesus and I talk, and sometimes I fuss. This was a fussing day. I was sitting in the line at Krystal's drive-through awaiting my chance to order another Roadie, and I was fussing at the Lord: "Lord, You got me into this thing with the faith promise. And I'm happy to do it. But I need a sign from You. Something I can understand. Just anything. I need to know how much I should trust You in this. And I just don't see where it is going to come from!" I was agitated and frustrated.

About that time, I heard: "Welcome to Krystal. Can I take your order?"

"I just want a Roadie unsweet iced tea," I said.

"Come on around, Pastor," came the reply.

As the familiar young lady was passing me my iced tea, she looked at me and politely said, "Can I ask you something?"

"Sure," I replied.

She paused for a second and then blurted out: "Don't your wife know how to brew tea?"

I started to say, "Well, yes . . . ," but she went on: "I mean, you're spending a lot of money on some unsweet tea, and I'm just thinking . . . well, aren't you a pastor?"

"Yes, you know I am," I said.

"Well, I'm just saying, don't you know that's God's money you're spending on all this tea?"

I got beat up by the drive-through lady at Krystal!

So, I put my tea in the cup holder and drove away. "Just a sign, Lord, anything . . ." I had prayed.

I'm ashamed to admit it, but as I was driving to the office that afternoon, I did some quick calculations in my head. I discovered that I was spending a little more than twelve hundred dollars a year on unsweet iced tea! And before any of you reading this judge me, I've got one word for you: *Starbucks!*

I honestly still didn't know how much our faith promise needed to be, but I knew it'd better be at least $1,200. The Lord had shown me that He had already provided that much in discretionary resources in our lives.

Our goal for that first faith promise offering was $75,000. I do believe the congregation as a whole took the process seriously. I think they listened and allowed the Lord to lead. When the results were tabulated, we learned that the congregation had committed $829,000! And even as I was celebrating the miraculous provision of God, provision that would forever change the mission outreach of that church, something else occurred to me: that amount represented eleven times our goal of $75,000 in our eleven-year-old church. It was as if God was saying, "You wanted $75,000 for My mission? I've had $75,000 in pent-up desire for every year that you didn't give My people a clear pathway to engage the mission!"

I've seen it over and over again through the years: there is provision when we are on mission.

There is power, purpose, and provision when we are on mission. And God wants each of His children to experience all of these things.

John Piper, pastor of Bethlehem Baptist Church in Minneapolis, also understands that mission is the reason the church exists. He is very direct in speaking about that mission. When it comes to the mission of Jesus, he says to Christ-followers: "You are either a passionate goer, a passionate sender, or you are passionately disobedient."

The Lord is still surveying this broken world and asking the same question He put before Isaiah: "Whom shall I send?" (Isa. 6:8a).

Why not consider making Isaiah's reply your own: "Here am I. Send me!" (v. 8b)? Your life will never be the same again if you do.

EIGHT

Your Deepest Desires

> *With this in mind, we constantly pray for you,*
> *that our God may make you worthy of his*
> *calling, and that by his power he may bring*
> *to fruition your every desire for goodness and*
> *your every deed prompted by faith.*
>
> —2 Thessalonians 1:11

It is true that mission is the reason the church exists, and there is no greater example of how to live out that missional calling than the very first missionary sent forth from the church: the apostle Paul. Although there was a point in Paul's life during which he was one of the most dangerous and feared opponents of the fledgling church, his dramatic experience with the risen Lord and his subsequent trust in Jesus as his Savior produced one of the most dramatic life changes ever seen. And it is remarkable how Paul's encounter with the Lord mirrors that of Isaiah.

Paul, or Saul as he was called in Hebrew, was born
to a devout Jewish family in Tarsus, a Roman city on
the coast of the Mediterranean. He descended from a
long line of devout Pharisees, practitioners of a strict
form of legalistic Judaism. At a young age, Saul was
given the opportunity to go to Israel and study with
the great rabbi Gamaliel. At the time, Gamaliel was a
member of the Jewish ruling council, the Sanhedrin,
and was considered by most to be the greatest rabbi
of his day. Saul had the benefit of Roman citizen-
ship by birth, strong standing in the global Jewish
community as a "Pharisee of Pharisees," and growing
respect from all as an accomplished student of the
great rabbi Gamaliel. Making the most of his advan-
tages, Saul began to establish a name for himself in
Judaism as a devout worshipper of God and defender
of the faith. And having been present at the stoning
of Saint Stephen—where a young Saul kept an eye on
the coats of those who were stoning the evangelist (see
Acts 7:58b)—Saul left that scene a determined persecutor of all followers of Jesus. He later pursued them to
foreign lands in order to bring them back to Jerusalem
for sentencing and death.

On one such trip, this time to Damascus, Saul's
life would change forever: "As he neared Damascus
on his journey, suddenly a light from heaven flashed
around him. He fell to the ground and heard a voice
say to him, 'Saul, Saul, why do you persecute me?'
'Who are you, Lord?' Saul asked. 'I am Jesus, whom
you are persecuting,' he replied" (Acts 9:3–5).

As with Isaiah, Saul saw the Lord in all His
glory. Indeed, the glory was so powerful that Saul
was blinded for three days by the experience. Unlike

Isaiah, however, Saul had not been looking for the Lord; Paul would later write that "he appeared to me" (1 Cor. 15:8a). Nevertheless, the effect was just as dramatic. When he saw the glory of the Lord, he immediately knew it was the Lord, and in the light of that glory, he also began to see himself as he truly was. Despite his blindness, Saul spent the next three days in total fasting and prayer, looking inward to come to terms with who he was and what he had done. We have seen how he later wrote that he did not even deserve to be called an apostle because of the depths of his sinfulness before his encounter with Jesus. Upon arriving in Damascus, however, Saul also had his grace experience. Describing his response to this grace, Paul wrote:

> For I am the least of the apostles and do not even deserve to be called an apostle, because I persecuted the church of God. But by the grace of God I am what I am, and his grace to me was not without effect. No, I worked harder than all of them—yet not I, but the grace of God that was with me. (1 Cor. 15:9–10)

And just as with Isaiah before him, Saul accepted the grace of God and believed that God had cleansed him. He also understood that God had done so for a purpose. He immediately began to prepare to serve Jesus, and would subsequently answer every missionary call put forth to him by God and His church for the rest of his life. As with Isaiah, Paul looked up and saw the Lord; he looked inward and saw himself as he really was; he looked outward and saw and embraced the grace of the Lord; and he looked around, recognized the need, and joined Jesus in His mission.

As a result, neither Paul's life—nor the world—would ever be the same again.

A Universal Calling

Paul understood full well that a missional response to the grace of God is not something reserved for a few super-Christians. From the earliest days of his missionary life, Paul took people with him, encouraged others to go out, and kept the call before the church.

In his second letter to the church in Thessalonica, Paul wants to encourage the Christ-followers in this young faith community. He opens his letter by praising the believers there for their growing faith and the increasing love they have for one another. He acknowledges that life has not been easy for them. These believers have undergone intense persecution and serious trials. Paul encourages them to persevere and assures them that God will one day set things right, and that when that day comes, those who are found faithful will also be found worthy of the kingdom of God. Then he shares with the church his prayer for them all: "With this in mind, we constantly pray for you, that our God may make you worthy of his calling, and that by his power he may bring to fruition your every desire for goodness and your every deed prompted by faith" (2 Thess. 1:11).

Paul's prayer acknowledges the universality of the calling of Jesus and paints an amazingly powerful and compelling picture of the fruit that can grow from living an empowered life worthy of that calling. He speaks from experience, having lived such a life while witnessing both the power and the fruitfulness. And he sincerely desires this life for every one of the believers in Thessalonica, and for all other disciples of Jesus as well. Let's look a little more deeply at this beautiful promise-filled prayer.

Worthy of His Calling

Paul is hopeful that the Lord might make us "worthy of his calling." But what does he mean by "his calling"? Fortunately, we don't have to speculate as to the calling of Jesus. Jesus was a first-century rabbi. As such, He called disciples. Jesus was not the only rabbi in His time who had disciples. Gamaliel, Paul's teacher, also had disciples, as did a number of other renowned rabbis of that era. Jesus was somewhat unique in His day, however, in that He went out and called His disciples. Matthew 4:19 gives us a portrait of that calling: "Come, follow me . . . and I will send you out to fish for people." Found within this simple call are the three critical elements of our calling.

First, Jesus says, "Come, follow me." This simple statement is an invitation that requires a decision and demands movement. During the earthly ministry of Jesus, there were some who heard these words and immediately got up and followed Jesus. There were others who made the decision that the price was too high, or the challenge too great, and rejected the invitation. One way or the other, however, the call asks for a decision. And it was not a decision to be made lightly.

In first-century Palestine, when a rabbi called a disciple, this calling was not an invitation to join a weekly Bible study, nor even a request to join a synagogue. Disciples lived in daily close proximity to their rabbis. They learned and imitated every aspect of their rabbi's life. In those days a blessing was commonly prayed over disciples which said, "May you be covered in the dust of your rabbi!" The idea was that the disciple would follow the rabbi so closely and so regularly that while walking along the dusty roads of Israel, the dust from the sandals of the rabbi would fall over the heads of the disciples.

The goal of discipleship was for these young students to become so familiar with the rabbi and his body of teaching that a disciple could, in turn, carry on the rabbi's teaching and model the life of the rabbi. Therefore, when Jesus says, "Come, follow me," He is not putting forth a casual invitation, but is proposing a significant and profound life commitment. That commitment is the same today as it was two thousand years ago.

The calling does not end with a decision to follow Jesus. In fact, that decision is only the beginning of a lifetime of discipleship. Jesus says, "and I will make you . . ." Following Jesus is not simply about going somewhere, or even learning some things. It is about being shaped and molded by our Rabbi. As we have already seen, this process of being made by Jesus is something the church calls "sanctification." The apostle Paul referred to it as moving from glory to glory into the image of Jesus (see 2 Corinthians 3:18). Sanctification is not something we do or something we earn. Instead, it is something God does in us and for us as we cooperate with Him and allow His grace, through the power of the Holy Spirit, to do its work in our lives. Paul wrote to the Church in Philippi concerning this process: "Continue to work out your salvation with fear and trembling, for it is God who works in you to will and to act in order to fulfill his good purpose" (Phil. 2:12b–13).

John Wesley believed that since it is grace that accomplishes this sanctifying work in the life of a disciple, it is best to regularly engage with the means of grace. Although the grace of God can be encountered and can do its complete work anywhere, there are some practices in which the grace of God flows more regularly and more predictably. Wesley divided these "means of grace" into two groupings. The first, "works of piety," refer to specific things that individual disciples are encouraged to practice regularly such as reading, meditating on, and studying the Bible; spiritual fasting; praying; attending worship services; and sharing faith with others. Additionally, works of piety include some things we do together with other Christ-followers. These include taking Communion, baptism, meeting together with other believers for mutual accountability in faith and practice, and studying the Bible in community.

Second, Wesley spoke of "works of mercy." These include individual acts such as caring for the sick, welcoming the stranger, visiting the imprisoned, feeding the hungry, and giving generously to the poor. Additionally, works of mercy also include things we do together with other Christ-followers, such as seeking justice, addressing the root causes of poverty, and working to end oppression in whatever forms it may take.

Regularly practicing these means of grace is a big part of following Jesus. As we attend to these means of grace, we can be sure that the Holy Spirit is operative in our lives, moving us from glory to glory into the image of Jesus (see 2 Corinthians 3:18). This is sanctification. It is putting ourselves into the hands of Jesus and allowing Him to "make" us (see 2 Thessalonians 1:11). And He is making us for a purpose.

The final part of Jesus' calling concerns the purpose for which we are being made. Jesus said, "I will make you fishers of [people]" (Matt. 4:19 NKJV). Because those to whom He was speaking were fishermen, Jesus was using language they would understand. But He is not literally talking about fishing here. Instead, He is letting His potential disciples know that they will move from what has been their mission in life, their work, into joining Him in His mission. Jesus made that even more explicit when He appeared to the disciples after His resurrection: "As the Father has sent me, I am sending you" (John 20:21b). He then breathed on them and filled them with the Holy Spirit. Jesus was saying to them, "My mission is now your mission, and the same power source that empowered My mission will now empower yours."

The Discipleship of Paul

We can see how all of these elements of the calling of Jesus play out in the personal discipleship of Paul. As he fixed his eyes upon Jesus and listened to the voice of the Holy Spirit, he moved through each of the stages of discipleship.

He saw his need for salvation and listened to Jesus his Savior. Saul had spent most of his life prior to his encounter with Jesus building a name and a reputation for himself. For the rest of his life, he would be able to point back to all his personal accomplishments, which were considerable. Yet, in the light of the glorified Jesus, he understood almost at once how insignificant all of his personal striving had been. He was broken and repentant. He knew he needed a savior and he understood that Jesus was that Savior, and that

Jesus was calling him! Paul would later write: "What is more, I consider everything a loss because of the surpassing worth of knowing Christ Jesus my Lord, for whose sake I have lost all things. I consider them garbage, that I may gain Christ" (Phil. 3:8).

It is fascinating to me to consider the day when Jesus appeared to Saul on the road to Damascus, and Saul met his Savior. There were several others on the road with Saul that day, and all of them were deeply religious people. Yet only Saul actually saw and heard Jesus. There are many religious people in the world who have become so self-confident in their own religious accomplishments and learnings that they can't even imagine needing a savior. They have embraced the rules of religion, but often miss the relationship with "the author and finisher of our faith" (Heb. 12:2 NKJV). In the light of Jesus' glory, Saul understood that, though educated and devout, he was spiritually blind and in need of a savior. He accepted the personal invitation to come follow Jesus.

Paul also saw his need to be remade and listened to Jesus his Maker. From the moment of his encounter with the living Jesus, Saul understood that he needed to be made in His image. He writes to the church in Galatia:

> But when God, who set me apart from my mother's womb and called me by his grace, was pleased to reveal his Son in me so that I might preach him among the Gentiles, my immediate response was not to consult any human being. I did not go up to Jerusalem to see those who were apostles before I was, but I went into Arabia. Later I returned to Damascus. (Gal. 1:15–17)

Indeed, scholars tells us that Paul spent the better part of the next nine years following Jesus and growing in his discipleship. This process of sanctification, which would be an ongoing part of Paul's life for the rest of his days, he describes to the Corinthians in this way: "And we all, who with unveiled faces contemplate the Lord's glory, are being transformed into his image with ever-increasing glory, which comes from the Lord, who is the Spirit" (2 Cor. 3:18). Because Paul had cooperated with his Maker in the process of being formed as a disciple, he could also say to the Corinthians: "Follow my example, as I follow the example of Christ" (1 Cor. 11:1).

Finally, Paul saw his need for direction and listened to Jesus his Lord. There are, sadly, many in the church today who desire a savior but really aren't interested in a Lord. Paul understood that the only acceptable response to the grace of God in Jesus Christ was to submit to Him as Lord. Following Jesus, for Paul, meant that the Lord's business became his business. As he joined Jesus in His mission in the world, Paul not only took direction from Jesus, he also found his hope in the Lord: "Brothers and sisters, I do not consider myself yet to have taken hold of it. But one thing I do: Forgetting what is behind and straining toward what is ahead, I press on toward the goal to win the prize for which God has called me heavenward in Christ Jesus" (Phil. 3:13–14).

We see the extent of Paul's willingness to subjugate his own plans to the will of his Lord in a defining episode from the book of Acts:

Paul and his companions traveled throughout the region of Phrygia and Galatia, having been kept by the Holy Spirit from preaching the word in the province of Asia. When they came to the border of Mysia, they tried to enter Bithynia, but the Spirit of Jesus would not allow them to. So they passed by Mysia and went down to Troas. During the night Paul had a vision of a man of Macedonia standing and begging him, "Come over to Macedonia and help us." (Acts 16:6–9)

To be certain, Paul made his own plans, and brought his best wisdom to bear on what he should be doing. But from the point of his encounter with Jesus, he became willing to adjust his plans to the promptings of the Lord.

Paul models for all Christ-followers the pattern of discipleship. He responded to the gracious call of Jesus and received Him as Savior. He cooperated with his Maker in the process of sanctification as the Spirit moved him from glory to glory into the very image of Jesus (see 2 Corinthians 3:18). And he submitted to Jesus his Lord as he joined Jesus in His mission in the world. Thus, he lived a life worthy of the calling of Jesus.

The Only Mission That Matters

We have talked a lot about joining Jesus in His mission. So, what, exactly, is that mission? In recent decades, parts of the church in North America have watered down the mission of Jesus until anyone who is doing anything even remotely helpful or is simply being nice to others is thought to be on mission. From its inception, however, the actual mission of Jesus has been about one thing: making disciples. Jesus spent

the entirety of His earthly ministry making disciples.
And as He gathered with His disciples on the evening
before He was crucified, He prayed to His heavenly
Father: "I have brought you glory on earth by finishing
the work you gave me to do" (John 17:4). It is essential to
note that Jesus had not yet been to the cross, much less
risen from the dead. He had much remaining work to
do. But He had made disciples. And it says something
about the importance the Lord places on disciple-
making that He would indicate that this was the work
His Father sent Him to do, and that by doing it, He had
brought glory to His Father on earth. How remarkable that Jesus would now entrust this God-glorifying
mission to us! Yet, that is exactly what He does.

The final words in Matthew's gospel have come
to be widely known as the Great Commission. It is
understood by the church that in these words Jesus is
giving marching orders to those who would join Him
in His mission:

> Then Jesus came to them and said, "All
> authority in heaven and on earth has been
> given to me. Therefore go and make disciples
> of all nations, baptizing them in the name
> of the Father and of the Son and of the Holy
> Spirit, and teaching them to obey everything
> I have commanded you. And surely I am
> with you always, to the very end of the age."
> (Matt. 28:18–20)

There is a command in these verses, and only one.
I have had the opportunity to share with communities
of believers in dozens of countries around the world,
and I commonly ask them: "What is the command in

the Great Commission?" Nearly 100 percent of the time the immediate and enthusiastic answer is: "Go!"

Many years ago, the late Christian singer Keith Green recorded a song entitled "Jesus Commands Us to Go." It is a beautiful song, and the song's sentiments are shared by many passionate believers. It is, however, also theologically incorrect. The Great Commission does not command us to go. We know this because the text is handed down to us in Greek, a language in which command verbs have their own form. When looking at this passage in Greek, it becomes clear: the only command in the entire passage is "make disciples." In fact, Jesus seems to assume that those who follow Him would not need to be commanded to go. Movement is more or less implied in the act of following. A better translation of this passage in English would be something like: "As you are going . . . make disciples!"

The mission of Jesus is to make disciples. Period. And while there are thousands and thousands of ways to make disciples, and we can utilize many platforms to accomplish this vital work, not everything that is nice and helpful is also disciple-making. It is essential that those who would live lives worthy of the calling of Jesus be about the work of making disciples. It is the only mission that ultimately matters, and the one that brings glory to God on the earth. And the good news is that we are not on our own as we live into this mission.

Paul reminds the believers in Thessalonica that it is the power of God that makes the mission possible. As we saw in the last chapter, there is power when we are on mission. Paul now prays for two incredible outcomes for those who would live lives worthy of the calling of Jesus. These outcomes are both accomplished "by his power" (see 2 Thessalonians 1:11).

Your Every Desire for Goodness

Paul says that by God's power "he may bring to fruition your every desire for goodness" (2 Thess. 1:11).
Wow! Stop and think about that for a moment. Have
you ever had a desire to do something good? I have
asked this question to groups large and small through
the years, and I have yet to meet anyone who said
no. Honestly, every four-year-old has had a desire to
do something good. It seems to be inborn in human
beings. Unfortunately, dream-killers, negative people,
and the brokenness of our fallen world often grind this
healthy desire out of people. And sometimes people
stop believing that they have it in them to bring forth
goodness. But Paul is holding out the radical possibility that for those living lives worthy of the calling
of Jesus, God is able to empower their desires for
goodness and bring them into full fruitfulness. How
wonderful could it be if the Lord were bringing to
fruitfulness not just a few good ideas, but every desire
for goodness His followers have?

Paul understood how God could do this very
thing. Shortly after the persecution that scattered the
early church in Jerusalem, the apostles and believers
who remained in the city fell on hard economic times.
Apparently, they were quite impoverished and living
in dire straits. Paul, as he traveled on his missionary
journeys, had a desire for goodness. He felt led to take
a collection among the new believers in the churches
he was planting to help with the impoverished mother
church in Jerusalem. He put out the word, and God
began to empower the work. As Paul was trying to

encourage the support of the church in Corinth in this project, he mentioned the faithfulness of the churches in Macedonia:

> In the midst of a very severe trial, their over-flowing joy and their extreme poverty welled up in rich generosity. For I testify that they gave as much as they were able, and even beyond their ability. Entirely on their own, they urgently pleaded with us for the privilege of sharing in this service to the Lord's people. (2 Cor. 8:2–4)

Do you see the power of God? How is it possible for a persecuted group of young believers, impoverished and undergoing trials, to give "even beyond their ability"? Only by the power of God. Paul's desire for goodness was brought to fruition by the power of God. And this happened over and over again. It is still happening today.

In the church where Fred launched his clown ministry, we operated with a permission-giving model of ministry development. If someone in the church felt called to launch a ministry, there was very little red tape required to make it happen. They were asked to create a mission statement (including an explanation of how the ministry would contribute to the making of disciples); they were charged with building a team (lone-ranger ministries can go weird quickly, which may be why Jesus did not send people out on their own to do ministry); the ministry had to be consistent with the mission and values of the local church; and they had to determine the funding sources for the ministry.

If those four requirements were fulfilled, anyone was free to launch any ministry prompted by the Holy Spirit and their desire for goodness.

I will never forget the day Nancy came to see me about what was on her heart. She had done some study on the meal opportunities for people in our community. She said, "Pastor, do you realize that hungry people can get a hot meal in this community on Tuesday, Thursday, Friday, Saturday, and Sunday, but Mondays and Wednesdays they are out of luck?" I confessed that I was not aware of that situation and asked her what she proposed we do about it.

"I'm glad you asked. I think we should start a feeding ministry in our Fellowship Hall on Mondays and Wednesdays. We can incorporate some other ministry elements for those who would be interested, and make it open for all hungry people to receive a meal. I already have some people who are willing to be involved with this ministry, and we have a mission statement. What do you think?"

It was clear to me that this ministry would also align with our church's mission and values, so I told Nancy that it sounded interesting. I asked her what would stop them from getting it going.

"Well, we have to find a source for the food, and we would need to open up a pass-through window between the kitchen and the Fellowship Hall, plus we would need to install a commercial-grade dishwasher and a couple of big freezers for the food. I figure getting all of that would require about $10,000. So, if you could see your way clear to get the church to approve the money, we could get going right away."

I reminded Nancy that part of our permission-giving approach to ministries was that the new ministries needed to have a funding source. She said she thought the church could be that funding source since clearly there was a community need. But I sensed that God was up to something bigger than this feeding ministry. I really believed that God wanted to demonstrate His power and provision, and to help Nancy's desire for goodness come to fruition. So, I said, "Nancy, let's pray and put this before the Lord and see what God does." She agreed to pray, though I think she was disappointed in my response. We put the need before the Lord and she reluctantly went home.

A week or so later, Nancy was back in my office. "Wow, God really showed up!" she said with renewed enthusiasm.

> I talked with one of the local grocery stores and they have agreed to let us have a number of bakery and produce items that they can't sell. They will give them to us at no cost twice weekly. That only left the meats, as far as food needs. Then I bumped into someone in a random conversation who told me about an operation out of Tampa who will not only supply meat to ministries like this, free of charge, but will deliver it in refrigerated trucks each week. And to make matters even better, Rudy [who was our resident contractor, handyman, and Mr. Fixit] has agreed to cut the pass-through into the fellowship hall, provide the needed supplies, and do all the finish work. He will also get the plumbing and electric worked up so that we are ready for the commercial dishwasher and the freezers. All free of charge.

I could sense Nancy's excitement, and I was excited too. It is always so wonderful to see the power of God at work. Then she said, "So, if you could just get the church to buy us the dishwasher and the freezers, we could get started! Can you do that?" The excitement left her eyes almost immediately when I said, "No, Nancy. God is doing amazing work. Let's pray again and see what happens." This time her prayers were even less enthusiastic than before, and I really think she was growing irritated with me. But we prayed, and she went on her way.

It was a couple of days later when Nancy came by to tell me about a chance encounter on the street in our small town.

> You know that restaurant that just closed? Well, I bumped into the lady that owned it. She told me that she had heard about what we were trying to do with the feeding program. She said that she was willing to give us their commercial dishwasher at no cost if we would come and get it and have it installed in our place. So, I talked to Rudy, and he's on his way to get it. He will hook it up tomorrow and we will be ready to go. All we need are a couple of freezers. Do you think the church could buy the freezers so we could get this thing going? It is so exciting!

Now, I want to be honest. We could easily have bought the freezers. In fact, we probably could have funded the whole thing right from the start. But God seemed to be leading us in a different way, and at this point I wasn't about to get in God's way. When I told Nancy that I wanted to pray, I seriously thought she was going to hurt me! I could tell she was now deeply annoyed with me. But we prayed and she went on home.

It wasn't more than a couple of hours later that my office phone rang. It was Nancy on the line. This was well before cell phones, and we all still used answering machines that blinked when we had a message. Nancy said, "Well, I got home, and my answering machine was blinking up a storm. I had three calls from people, all offering me freezers for free. We only need two. Do you need a freezer?" We celebrated God's goodness over the phone, and agreed to launch the ministry the following week. Her team flew into action, and from then on, hungry people in our community could get a meal every day of the week.

It is true that we could have just written a check and started the work. But in allowing God to do this thing in His power, we not only clearly saw the hand of God's provision in the work, we also involved scores of people throughout the community who had bought into the mission and been used by God to play a role. That community enthusiasm helped to sustain the ministry long after Nancy's role in launching it had concluded. And God had, once again, brought to fruition Nancy's desire for goodness. It is what God does. And it is a common occurrence when Jesus' disciples are living lives worthy of His calling and joining Him in His mission.

Think for a moment about what your community, your church, and the world might be like if just your own desires for goodness were brought to fruition. Now multiply that by the multitudes of obedient believers, and it is easy to imagine the kingdoms of this world becoming the kingdom of our Lord and of His Christ.

Your Every Deed Prompted by Faith

Paul is not finished with his good news for the church at Thessalonica, nor for us. He goes on to say that by God's power He can also bring to fruition our "every deed prompted by faith" (2 Thess. 1:11). The great apostle is no stranger to steps of faith. He states clearly to the church in Corinth: "For we live by faith, not by sight" (2 Cor. 5:7). And Paul fully expects that believers who step with faith into the mission of Jesus will see their steps empowered by God. Time and again, Paul and his companions step into the mission in faith and speak before kings and jailers, receptive audiences and enraged mobs, synagogue leaders and church leaders, sinners and saints, and each time they see the power of God bringing fruitfulness from their endeavors. And, as with our desires for goodness, the Lord is still bringing fruitfulness to our steps of faith today.

Sunday, December 26, 2004, Boxing Day, was unlike any other in recent history. We in the West awoke to the news that hours earlier a massive undersea earthquake had unleashed deadly tsunamis all over the Indian Ocean. Before it was over, nearly 230,000 people lost their lives and millions more were displaced from Indonesia to Thailand to South Africa. The images that greeted me that morning as I prepared for our Sunday worship service were horrific. It was one of the most deadly and devastating natural disasters in modern history. And I knew the Christ-followers who gathered that morning for worship would want to, would actually need to, do something. It was time for a step of faith.

We had heard from a ministry partner in Southeast Asia who reported that while he and his people were okay, there was utter destruction in many places in his country and others around him. He had already priced out a box of relief supplies that would care for a family of four, complete with food, water, shelter, bedding, and some first aid supplies, for up to two weeks. He let us know that any funds we could raise would be immediately put to work in the devastated villages along the coast. As I was praying about this situation, I began to wonder aloud if God wanted to reproduce a miracle. I remembered the story of how Jesus had fed the five thousand men and their families on that Galilean hillside one afternoon by simply asking the people to bring him what they had. He blessed it and shared it, and not only was it enough, there were twelve baskets of food left over (see Matthew 14:13–21). A similar miracle seemed to be needed that morning.

As I opened the worship service, I acknowledged the tragedy we had all seen. We spoke about the need for prayer, and how our hearts were breaking for the people in Southeast Asia. Then I explained to the congregation about the boxes of relief supplies. I told them that we had calculated what it would cost to provide five thousand boxes, so that five thousand families could be rescued. Then I suggested that, although they had not come prepared for what we were about to do, I thought the Lord wanted us to bring Him what we already had, and see if He could bless it and feed those five thousand families. I proposed that we start with the front row and have each person come forward and put whatever money they brought with them that morning on the altar. And to start it all off, I took my wallet out and removed the money I had there (I had chosen a good day for this, as I think I only had twenty-three dollars that morning)

and placed it on the altar. Everyone just sort of looked
at me awkwardly and no one moved. So, I explained:
"This is not a theoretical exercise. My money is on the
table." Then I pointed at the gentleman sitting right
on the front row. "You're next." I held my breath as he
paused for just a second, but then got up and brought
his money to the table. One by one, the rest of the
congregation followed. The pile of money on the table
grew. Finally, when everyone had come down front,
the ushers gathered the money that had been given
and headed off to count it, while I preached to a very
generous, if somewhat subdued congregation. Just as
we were wrapping up the service, the ushers brought
a report. The congregation had given an amount that
was only twenty-nine short of the amount needed to
feed five thousand families. I told them I would add a
check for the remainder, and we would see what God
wanted to do. There was much celebration!

When the time came to distribute the aid boxes,
our team went into a fishing village at the end of a
peninsula where the entire village had been destroyed
by the tsunami. The beleaguered survivors in this
village were sitting among the destruction; everything
they had once known was gone. As we began to deliver
the aid boxes, the people in the village started to ask
who we were and why we were there. The government of the Southeastern Asian country had asked all
teams to please deliver the aid, but not to proselytize.
They were concerned about adding religious tensions
to an already chaotic situation. In trying to comply,
our team was simply saying things like, "We are here
because we love you," or, "We wanted to show you that
God loves and cares for you." But the village leaders
and elders were having none of it.

One particular elder said firmly, "Look around. No one else is here. No one ever comes here. The government doesn't come here. No one cares about us!" Then he raised his voice and asked again, "Why are you here?" One of our team replied, "It is because of Jesus." And the elder who had asked the question said, "Jesus, who?" We would discover after some conversation that in 2004 the name of Jesus had never been spoken in this village. The Savior of the world was completely unknown to them.

Later that day our team sat the people in the village down and shared the good news of Jesus Christ with them. When we were finished, that same elder came forward and said, "We are grateful for the supplies you have brought us. And we are grateful for this good news. And we believe this good news. And we believe that it is for us. But I do have a question: If Jesus lived two thousand years ago, as you say, and if this good news is for us, as you say, then why has it taken two thousand years for someone to care enough about us to bring us this message?" I didn't have an answer for that man that day, and to be honest, I don't have an answer for that even now. It is a good question.

We planned for some people to continue visiting the village, not only bringing relief, but sharing more with them about Jesus. Before too long, many people in the village had become followers of Jesus. They asked us if they could have a church building in their village. This created a bit of a dilemma. We had told them nothing about denominations, or ordination, or any kind of church polity. We were simply sharing the good news of Jesus and the Word of God. The last thing we wanted to get into with them was denominationalism or church rules. So, we did something a

bit unusual. We asked the elders if they had a young
couple who were intelligent and promising, but had not
decided yet what to do with their lives. They quickly
pointed to one young man and his new bride. Then
we asked the elders, "If we sent this young couple to a
Bible college for one year, when they return, would you
receive them as your pastors?" All of the people agreed
that they would, with gladness. The young couple, for
whom this was all quite a surprise, nonetheless agreed
to go to the Bible college. While they were away, we
arranged for a small church building to be built in
the village. Just as it was being completed, the young
couple returned to the village and we consecrated the
church and installed this young man as pastor.

The new young pastor was enthusiastic and hard-
working, and before too long, nearly 68 percent of the
people in the village had been baptized and were regularly participating in the life of the church. But the
church had also attracted the attention of some people
from a village back up the peninsula toward town.
Soon we received a call wanting to know if we could
come and build a church in the neighboring village.
My immediate response was "No! You build them a
church. We built one for you. Do the same for them.
And ask the elders of the village if there is a young
couple of promise who might be willing to go to Bible
college for a year!" The believers in the first village
were surprised to learn that they were allowed to build
a church in the next village. But they did, and we were
able to install a pastor there as well.

In 2013, almost ten years after the tsunami, I had
the opportunity to visit that first church in the original
village. It was a great celebration, and the people of
the village testified to not only how they had embraced

the good news, but how the gospel had impacted their village life in countless ways. But I felt even greater joy in realizing that, as we had driven out of the peninsula to get to the village, we had passed by six other churches, all established in the same way, all thriving and giving much-needed life to their villages and the people. Seven vital churches in less than a decade, all the fruit of one simple step of faith. By the power of God, He was bringing it all to fruition, just as He always does.

Mission is the reason the church exists. Every follower of Jesus in the church is called to join Jesus in His mission. The Lord empowers the mission and also uses it to help bring about the abundant life in and through His followers. My prayer for the church today is the same as Paul's was for the people in Thessalonica: that we might live lives worthy of the calling of Jesus, that by His power He might bring to fruition our every desire for goodness and our every deed prompted by faith. May it be so!

Everything You Need

Continue to work out your salvation with fear and trembling, for it is God who works in you to will and to act in order to fulfill his good purpose.

—Philippians 2:12b–13

Perhaps you have heard the story of the Sunday school teacher who was questioning her third graders one morning: "I'm thinking of something that has a long bushy tail, gathers nuts for the winter, and lives in nests in the treetops. Can anyone tell me what it is?"

One little boy anxiously waved his hand in the air. When the teacher recognized him, he excitedly replied, "Teacher, I know it is Jesus, because the answer is always Jesus. But I have to tell you, it sounds a lot like a squirrel!"

It is a cute story. And although the teacher was describing a squirrel, the little boy had also hit upon an important truth: the answer is always Jesus. If we

want to experience abundant life, the answer is Jesus.
If we want to enter the kingdom of God, the answer is
Jesus. If we want to come to know our purpose and
live the lives we were created to live, the answer is
Jesus. So, we fix our eyes on Jesus, and in doing so, we
discover that the focus of our gaze really does determine the state of our being. Forever.

The good news is that Jesus wants to know us, and
to be known by us. And He wants to show us the way to
the abundant life, the way to the kingdom, and the way
to our heavenly Father. On the last full evening with
His disciples before He went to the cross, Jesus shared
His love with them. He assured His followers that
He was going to prepare a place for them and would
return to take them to that place, so that they could be
with Him. "You know the way to the place where I am
going," He told them (John 14:4). But Thomas, one of
His disciples, said, "Lord, we don't know where you are
going. How can we know the way?" (v. 5).

"Jesus answered, 'I am the way and the truth and
the life. No one comes to the Father except through
me. If you really know me, you will know my Father
as well. From now on, you do know him and have seen
him'" (vv. 6–7).

Some years ago, I met with the very large family
of a dear woman from my church who had passed
away. As I was chatting with one of the granddaugh-
ters, I learned that this young woman was the personal
assistant to a famous Hollywood director. During
the conversation she mentioned that they would be
filming a major motion picture in Baltimore in the
coming months. As it turned out, I was also going
to be in Baltimore at that time, visiting my sister-in-
law who lived there. When this enthusiastic young

lady discovered that I would be in the city during the filming, she suggested that I drop by: "It would be nice to see you again, and you could watch some of the filming and meet the director." It sounded like fun, so we made the arrangements.

A few months later, I had the pleasure of visiting an abandoned Baltimore shopping mall that had been converted for the purposes of the movie. I was fascinated by the behind-the-scenes look at the filming process, and enjoyed meeting some of the actors and crew. The famous director was quite busy, and I had only seen him from a distance. When the entire team took a break for lunch, however, my host brought me over to introduce me. As we approached the director, she said, "This is Max. He's visiting Baltimore, and wanted to meet you." The director looked up a bit uncertainly, as if trying to understand who I was and why I was there. "I'm sorry, who are you?" he asked, pleasantly but with some confusion. Suddenly, before I could say anything, a flicker of recognition flashed across his face. "Oh, wait, you are the Jesus guy!" he said with a chuckle.

Now it was my turn to be confused. I just sort of looked at the director in surprise. He laughed again, and said, "I just remembered that my assistant mentioned you would be coming by today. She said she met you at her mother's funeral. I guess you must be a pastor." He chuckled again, and said, "She told me, 'I have never met anyone who talks about Jesus like this guy does. It is all the time. And he talks about Jesus like he knows Him. My family and I started calling him 'the Jesus guy.' So, nice to meet you, Jesus guy!"

To be honest, I think the director found the whole thing amusing. I'm not sure he meant his story as a compliment. But to me, it was the greatest compliment anyone had ever given me. "The Jesus Guy" is a label I am more than pleased to receive and a name I will willingly bear. I imagine the famous director thought I was impressed with him. I did enjoy meeting him, but I was not impressed. I considered meeting him as nothing at all compared to the wonder of knowing and being in relationship with my Lord Jesus. And I talk about Jesus as if I know Him because I do know Him. He is everything to me. The good news is: you can know Him too.

It Is All about Loving Relationship

When all is said and done, everything the Lord does for us, everything the Lord does in us and through us, every God-encounter in our lives, is about relationship. We were created for relationship with God and with each other. The Great Commandment is all about healthy, loving relationship with God and with others. The cross itself is God's ultimate act of love. The Lord went first to bridge the relational chasm sin created between human beings and their Creator. By His grace, the Lord has been pursuing us with His love for our entire lives, going before us in an attempt to woo us to Himself.

Sometimes we get the wrong idea about God's desire to be in relationship with His creation. We feel put upon by being asked to follow Him. We might even see the idea of pursuing the Lord as a duty, an unpleasant obligation to a demanding God. But loving relationship can never be forced, only chosen. Thus, at times, God allows us to wander away, to focus our gaze on lesser things, and to seek abundant life from other sources. Then, when absence truly does make the heart grow fonder, when we come to see that nothing other than the Lord will fill that God-shaped void in our lives, and when we finally turn our gaze back toward Him, we discover that He has been there all along, continuing to pursue us with His grace.

We look up, and we see the glory of God. But we only see God's glory because He has been seeking us all along. His prevenient grace has gone before us from the moment we were conceived. The Lord has made us aware of who He is, and chosen to reveal Himself to us. He has sought us out in our hiding places, and drawn us to His light. When I returned home after becoming a Christ-follower, one of the men in the church in which I had grown up said to me, "Young man, you never had a chance. Your father and several of us men were praying regularly for you. And the hound of heaven was on your trail. You didn't find Him; He found you!" In that moment, I knew this man was telling it true.

We look inward, and we see ourselves as we really are. But we only see the truth because the Lord is shining the light of His love into the secret places of our lives. His convicting grace is working within us, reminding us of the tarnished image of God that is still present in our lives. His grace allows us to see what our lives could be, what our lives were meant to be. And in the dawning awareness that we were created to be so much more than we are, we find the courage to come clean with our Maker, and reorient our lives toward Him.

We look outward, and discover the gracious love of God in Jesus Christ. But we only see the forgiveness and unconditional love of our Lord because the Lord went first. He atoned for our sins while we were still sinners, and took upon Himself the punishment for our sins (see Romans 5:8). His justifying grace enables us to be pronounced clean. And the power of the Holy Spirit enables our own spirit to trust and believe that we are who the Lord says we are.

And even when we look around and discover the need, the mission of Jesus, and our place in it, we are really only seeing those good works that God prepared beforehand for us to walk in. His sanctifying grace enables Him to restore the image of God within us, one day at a time, and to begin to shape us for the lives we were created to live. It is in living those lives that we come to understand what the abundant life truly is.

As we fix our eyes upon Him, we discover that we can only do so because He has had His brilliant gaze fixed upon us all along. While our love is fickle, His love never fails.

God Does Not Need Us

Even in the light of God's grace, we can get the idea that God's mission in the world is dependent upon us, our actions, and obedience. Sometimes this attitude is expressed by those who say, "Pray as if everything depends on God, and then work as if everything depends on you." In reality, we should pray as if everything depends on God, and then work as if everything depends on God. Because everything depends on God. The idea that God needs us is a misconception of both who God is and why God desires to include us in His mission in the world.

As we have already noted, the Lord spoke the universe into being. He created the heavens and the earth unassisted. History is His story, and God is fully capable of bringing it to the consummation He has already ordained without the help of anyone or anything in creation. The simple truth is: God does not need us.

When my children were very young, my family lived in a house on a lake in a small Florida town. We loved the house, but it came with a 2.5-acre lawn almost entirely devoid of trees. Grass grows rapidly in the hot and humid Florida summers, and for many months I was forced to mow that lawn a couple of times per week. Even with a nice riding tractor, it typically took me four to five hours to finish the job.

One hot summer day, I was preparing to cut the lawn when I looked up and saw my three-year-old son Joshua standing on the porch, watching me. Just as I was ready to get started, he threw his arms up in the air, and said, "Daddy, I want to help." He stood there smiling, wide-eyed, expectantly waiting for me to pick him up and put him in my lap so that he could help me cut the lawn.

Of course, I did not need my three-year-old son's help that afternoon. I was bigger, stronger, and perfectly able to navigate the lawn tractor without his assistance. I had brought him into the world and spent the better part of the prior three years making sure his every need was met. He was utterly dependent upon me not only for his sustenance, but pretty much for his very existence. How ridiculous for him to assume that I needed anything from him. Despite all of that, I was absolutely delighted by his desire to help.

I immediately said, "Come over here, son," and I carefully lifted him into my lap. Then, securing him there, I placed his hands on the steering wheel of the tractor, wrapped my arms carefully around his, and very slowly proceeded to cut the lawn with his help. Of course, we had to go much more slowly than usual along the banks of the lake and around the obstacles. We needed several breaks for water and refreshment, as the hot sun took its toll on a three-year-old much more rapidly than it did on me. Yet we worked patiently together and completed the job. That familiar task, which normally took me four to five hours to complete, only took me six-and-a-half hours with my son's help. And I loved every minute of it!

Obviously, I did not need my son's help that day. But that is beside the point. It really was not about completing the task. It was all about the relationship. While I didn't need his help, I wanted his love. I desired to be in relationship with him. And my heart was made glad because he wanted to be in relationship with me. He wanted to be part of something he knew I found important. He didn't really want to cut that grass either. He wanted to be present with his father, he wanted to join his father in meaningful activity, and he wanted to experience his father's acceptance and love. Neither of us was acting out of obligation. Both of us treasured the moment, and all the subsequent moments where a relationship of love was our reason for being.

God doesn't need us. God doesn't need our help. But God wants us! The Lord desires our relationship. He wants our love. He wants to share the richness of His love with us. And our heavenly Father's heart is made glad when His children come to Him and, with their eyes firmly fixed on Him, raise their arms and say,

"Daddy, I want to help." It is never about the task. It is always about the relationship. It is one of the greatest acts of God's grace when He wraps His arms of love around us, pulls us to Himself, and moves together with us into whatever life has brought our way. These are the moments when life is most abundant.

ACKNOWLEDGMENTS

No one ever writes a book in a vacuum. Everything that ends up on paper is a product of numerous influences, both large and small, from countless people throughout the author's lifetime. I am deeply grateful for the impact my relationships have had on my life and the ways each one has shaped my story. Although I am not able to thank everyone by name, I appreciate each of them.

There are three men who have had a profound effect on my life and ministry. Each one has given of himself, unselfishly, in mentoring relationships at various stages of my journey. In choosing to invest in me, they have imparted gifts more valuable than gold. If there is anything praiseworthy in my life, it is in large part due to the example and influence of these men.

The Reverend Dr. Odell Miley took a raw, immature, fledgling pastor straight out of seminary and helped me, through words of wisdom and a personal example, to understand what a decades-long life of faithfulness in ministry looks like. His example continues to inspire me, and his constant love is a source of great encouragement.

Bishop Dick Wills, while pastoring a large, prevailing church, made time weekly for years to meet with me (and others), encouraging us in leadership, ministry, and vision. Dick is also a fount of wisdom and a constant source of encouragement—always without a hint of self-interest. Decades later, I still draw from his counsel on an almost weekly basis.

Pastor Wayne Cordeiro, while pastoring one of the fastest-growing and most fruitful churches in America, made the time to mentor hundreds of pastors and leaders from all over the world. I count it as one of my life's greatest blessings that I had the good fortune to be one of those pastors. I know of no one who exudes more wisdom, more vision, and more pastoral encouragement than Pastor Wayne. Nearly every day for the last twenty-two years something I learned from Pastor Wayne has encouraged me, or challenged me, or, in some profound way, shaped the way I have lived out my calling.

I will always be grateful for the influence of these three mentors.

I am also indebted to TMS Global's Senior Director of Communications Ruth Burgner for her significant role in getting this book ready for publication. Ruth is the most encouraging person I know, with a deep and abiding faith, a love for the written word, immense skills as an editor, and a wonderful grace-filled and supportive personality. We have shared long conversations on the writing process, theology, and how best to communicate. Ruth was gracious enough to read through several drafts of this book, offering editorial and theological insights that have undoubtedly improved the whole work. And, as always, she has done so with immeasurable encouragement. I am grateful for Ruth's relentless support.

Finally, I have been blessed to work with the Seedbed team. J. D. Walt, Andrew Miller, and Andrew Dragos have devoted themselves to seeing this project to completion. I am grateful for their shepherding. Holly Jones worked faithfully to clean up my writing and get everything edited and ready for publication. I am thankful for her giftedness and her assistance. I am so happy to be a part of the Seedbed family as we work together to sow for the great awakening.